AF593288

THE GREYHOUND OWNER'S ENCYCLOPAEDIA

THE

The Greyhound Owner's

ENCYCLOPAEDIA

IVY M. REGAN

PELHAM BOOKS

First published in Great Britain by
PELHAM BOOKS LTD
44 Bedford Square
London WC1B 3DU
September 1975
Second impression March 1976
Second edition 1981

ISBN 0 7207 1348 X

Printed in Great Britain by
Hollen Street Press Ltd at Slough
and bound by Redwood Burn Ltd, Esher, Surrey

ACKNOWLEDGEMENTS

I would like to offer my grateful thanks to Mrs Judy de Casembroot, Mr Frank Schock (from sunny Australia), Mrs Idella Smith and Mr Happy Stutz for helpful information regarding their friend – the greyhound.

I would also like to thank Mr F. J. Underhill, Secretary of the National Greyhound Racing Club, for permission to use the article on Chromatography, and Mr G. P. T. Shotton, Racing Manager of Brighton and Hove Stadium, for permission to use his article on the Photo-finish which originally appeared in the *Brighton and Hove Stadium News.* My thanks too to the National Greyhound Racing Club Ltd for permission to reproduce from their rules; to the National Coursing Club for permission to use extracts from their Book of Rules; to the Kennel Club for permission to reproduce their Standard for Greyhounds, and to the Glaxo Laboratories for their advice on the medical treatment of greyhounds.

Ivy M. Regan

ILLUSTRATIONS

List of line drawings

Abortion: Fortunately not common in greyhounds, for abortion is dangerous in canines owing to the foetus being carried in the horns of the uterus and not in the uterus itself. It is essential to remove the foetuses by Caesarean operation.

Abscess: Containing pus, this may appear in any part of the body, from a variety of causes through the introduction of dirt organisms. Symptoms are a rise in temperature and the swelling of the affected area, through the presence of pus. Hot fomentations and hot poultices will bring the abscess to a head. (*See* ACCIDENTS.)

Accidents: Cuts, bites and wounds, even if severe, heal best if left to themselves – and the dog – without stitching. Keep the wound clean and apply Acraflavin emulsion liberally. Sold by some chemists as Proflavin, this is an antiseptic, and will remove dirt and loose hair, and is a great healer. It will not harm the dog if he licks this. In the case of a severe accident an animal, in its wild state, will find a place where he can lie, going without food for days if necessary to avoid getting up to evacuate, and then emerge cured. The great healing properties in his saliva will normally heal the wounds as he licks them.

Acclimatisation: (*see* ALTITUDE).

Affix: (Prefix). A name chosen by the owner or breeder of a dog registered with the Kennel Club, for breeding and show purposes of the exhibition greyhound; with the National Coursing Club for breeding and coursing purposes; and with the National Greyhound Racing Club for racing greyhounds.

On payment of a fee the name is registered for the sole use of the owner, unless that owner gives permission for one of his or her dogs to retain that name in changing ownership.

Afterbirth: (*see* PLACENTA).

Age for Racing: (*see* AGE OF A GREYHOUND). Since greyhound racing first started in England and Ireland, the rule for assessing the age of a racing greyhound was the very worst in the governing book. Any law, or rule, which invites cheating can only be bad – and this rule certainly did that. For years the English and Irish *Stud Books* abounded with January litters although January litters are, in fact, fairly uncommon.

Under the old rule, irrespective of the month of arrival, the greyhound racing authorities took 1 January in the year of his birth as his birth date. This meant that puppies born in the latter part of the year were classed as two-year-olds before they had actually reached the age of fifteen months, when they were officially eligible to start racing under NGRC rules.

Some years ago the major puppy races, with the exception of the September Produce Stakes, were run from November until very late December; but in recent years, starting with Wembley's Trafalgar Cup in August, they have taken place much earlier. This meant that a puppy born after May had no chance in competing in these, as he would not be old enough to start racing.

Even when he reached that age, under NGRC rules, he had to have three official trials on his Identity Book before competing in a race, and these were not allowed to start until he reached his fifteenth month. This meant that a great many puppies born in the latter part of a year went in as January whelps of the next year for, on payment of an extra fee, a puppy could be registered at six months and veterinary surgeons openly stated that once a puppy went through his first teething stage, it was by no means easy to tell the exact age within some weeks.

Happily, this rule (since November 1972) has been changed. From this date a greyhound puppy has the uncomplicated pleasure of being only as old as he is.

Age of a Greyhound: For racing or coursing, a puppy's birthday is counted as the first day of the month in which it is born. Until the greyhound is two years old, he is counted as a puppy. The minimum age at which it can run on an NGRC racecourse is fifteen months. (*See* AGE FOR RACING.)

Almond Oil: (*see* EAR CARE).

Altitude: Greyhounds which are housed and trained at a high altitude will, at first, have a distinct advantage when competing against dogs trained at a lower altitude, but this advantage will last only for forty-eight hours after leaving their home ground. After this time, at the lower elevation, the reserves of oxygen stored up by them through living at a high altitude will be used up and they will become lethargic and, although they may seem to have settled in at their new surroundings, any performance by them which requires energy will be well below par. A dog from lower to higher ground would also be adversely affected, after forty-eight hours.

During the last few years the question of altitude, regarding racing animals, has been researched thoroughly, and time to acclimatize must be allowed – to ensure the best results – unless the racing or coursing can be completed within forty-eight hours.

An example of this is shown in the result of the 1973 Spanish Greyhound Derby. For nine years English greyhounds have competed in each Spanish Derby, all running below their known form. This year the English greyhounds competed but were taken to Spain a month before the competition, to give them time to acclimatize. The final was won by an English greyhound for the first time, with three English entries competing in the final. (*See* SPANISH GREYHOUND DERBY 1973.)

America, Racing in: There is no governing body, in the United States of America, which is exactly comparable with Britain's National Greyhound Racing Club, or Ireland's Bord nag Con, as these two organizations are fully supervisory. In America, all tracks belong to an organization called the American Greyhound Track Operators Association (AGTOA), which is more of a protective political body ensuring that their profits are not endangered by extra taxes, etc. There were forty-seven operative greyhound tracks in America in 1979.

Bookmaking is illegal in the USA and a law which is strictly enforced carries heavy penalties if broken. Although the method of racing is fairly similar to that in Britain and Ireland, the outcome is vastly different. All wagering on greyhound racing, as in horse racing, must go through the tote. As the tracks are privately owned, and vast profits may be made, a very large percentage of this money is ploughed back into the sport. This results in prize money being very high. Further, the facilities and amenities for patrons attending a top track in America are the finest in the world. Amounts invested on the tote in one night, at a major racecourse, will often approach and, at times, exceed one million dollars. At this type of track twelve races are run at each meeting with, as is usual in America, eight greyhounds in each race.

Only thirteen of the American States so far permit greyhound racing. Each track is allotted a racing season of sixty to one hundred and ten days each year, to run continuously. The number of racing days in each session will vary in the different States, as the governing laws are administered by each individual State. The leading tracks in America are: three in the vicinity of Boston, Mass.; four in the area of Miami, Florida; one in St Petersburg, Florida; one in Tampa, Florida; one in Memphis, Tenn.; one in Denver, Colorado; one in Phoenix, Arizona; and one in Portland, Oregon.

These thirteen tracks all have a nightly attendance of 10,000 or more. The average nightly betting at each of these tracks is in excess of half a million dollars.

Prize money is determined by the amount of money wagered at the entire meeting; of which two per cent is distributed as follows: 50 per cent to the winner, 25 per cent to the second dog, 15 per cent to the third dog and 10 per cent to the fourth dog. The top graded dogs receive double the amount of prize money of the lower graded dogs. On a major track the average purse for the top graded races will be one thousand to fifteen hundred dollars for each race – divided four ways, as above. In addition to the nightly purses most of these tracks will present at least one main stakes race (what we would call an 'open' race) and prize money may be as much as over thirty-five thousand dollars to the winner. For grading, the greyhounds are divided into six classes, which are designated by letters A,B,C,D,E and M. The M is for Maiden, the class where all young dogs start their careers. The dogs progress one letter at a time by winning, until they reach the top grade A. After a dog then finishes out of the prize money for three consecutive races (not being placed 1st, 2nd or 3rd) he is lowered one grade.

Most tracks have kennel and training facilities on adjacent property which, for a considerable fee, may be rented by Kennel Operators (comparative with trainers in England and Ireland). Some of the bigger operators have their own kennel establishment, with extensive grounds, training facilities and accommodation for as many as a hundred greyhounds. Mr 'Happy' Stutz, with a large training establishment in Florida, is well known in England and other countries for his help in promoting the sport internationally.

There are no quarantine restrictions for greyhounds entering America.

American-English Racing: At America's twelve-race greyhound meetings there are eight runners in each race competing for the highest prize money in the greyhound world. England's races field only six greyhounds, but a 1980 amendment to the English betting laws now permits ten races at each meeting, instead of the former eight. Further, on six special days in each year twenty-race sessions are allowed.

Amplex (veterinary): These tablets – obtainable from all chemists – are a very easy and acceptable way of removing the worry of bitches 'in season' (if they are not to be mated). Whilst it is not safe to leave a bitch and dog together at this time – even when giving the tablets – it will keep the dogs from realizing that there is a bitch in season kennelled nearby. Dose for greyhound bitch is 2 tablets three times a day.

Anaemia: Deficiency of blood or in the required number of its red corpuscles. Can be due to an insufficient or improper food supply, to repeated haemorrhages, or the inability to assimilate food.

Symptoms: The mucous lining of the eyelids, gums and mouth are pale and, in advanced cases, there is wasting and loss of energy.

Treatment: Easily digested food – such as underdone or raw meat. Bone marrow should be given (in the form of Virol).

If the dog shows symptoms of worms, he should be treated for them.

Anal Glands: When a dog is seen dragging his hindquarters along the ground – frequently licking the anus and tucking his tail in, it is usually due to the glands on each side of the anus filling with fluid which causes irritation, and should be removed. As a rule all that is required is to squeeze the glands, to evacuate the contents, then wiping with a piece of clean cotton wool first soaked in warm water to which a little boracic acid has been added. With some dogs it is necessary to give this treatment every few weeks.

Antibiotics: These are widely used in combating disease, and pencillin is perhaps one of the most well-known. A qualified veterinary surgeon should be called for the use of these. They are all obtained on prescription only and should *never* be used lightly. The vet will know for how long these should be carried on and the correct amounts to be given. If used in cases where they are not really necessary, although they may do no harm, they would not be so effective if they had to be used again for the same patient without a long enough time-lapse. When Sir Alexander Fleming, who discovered penicillin, was asked why it was not used for the common cold, he replied: 'One does not kill a fly with a sledgehammer!' This short, but vital, sentence tells us that this great man did not give penicillin alone to the world – for his invaluable advice, regarding the use of antibiotics, came with it. We know drugs have side effects, although often of less danger to the patient than the disease they are used for, but a dog has no choice of refusal. It is up to his keeper to see that he is not given a powerful drug for what can be diagnosed as a minor complaint.

Anus: The outlet of the rectum.

Anus, Prolapsis of: Although this may occur in adult dogs, it is more often seen in young puppies, usually the result of straining caused by diarrhoea or constipation. The lower bowel or rectum protrudes from the body and, if not relieved, becomes inflamed and swollen. The protruding part should be returned as quickly as possible. Vaseline the part and, holding the dog up by the hind legs, apply firm pressure to the prolapsis with the fingers, and it will then slip in. Avoid further constipation and, if necessary, give a mild laxative such as olive oil or medicinal paraffin. If the case is of long standing the prolapsis could occur again, in which case consult your vet.

Appetite, Depraved or Morbid: When dogs eat their own and other animals' excrement this is said to be due to worms, lack of vitamins, etc., but some of the dogs said to have this objectionable habit look in the peak of condition. Despite treating for worms and special feeding, the habit still persists. It is said that if the dog is muzzled for a time he may forget the habit, or else cayenne pepper dusted over something he might pick up will act as a deterrent – but still no one seems to be certain of the cause of this trouble.

An explanation, which seems feasible, was given to me a short time ago by someone who has studied dogs and their habits for many years. He said this goes back to when dogs lived in a wild state, and really had to search, and also travel, for their food, and this also explains why a dog always runs to where another dog has stopped.

By inspecting the motion of another dog, this dog could tell what the other had eaten, how long ago, and from which direction he had come. If he found the traveller had recently eaten a meal he would go back in the direction indicated by smell; but if he found there had been a very long journey without food he went on or, at least, in another direction. The hunter on his journey, not wishing to be followed, would often eat his excrement to prevent this.

Approved and Licensed Racecourses: Licensed under the Betting and Lotteries Act (1934) and most of them approved for greyhound racing by the NGRC Ltd. Independent tracks, even if not under the jurisdiction of the NGRC have to be licensed by the local authority.

Arsenic Poisoning: (*see* POISONS, ARSENIC).

Australia, Racing in: As in many other countries, greyhound or 'tin hare' racing, as it was called in Australia, was thought of long before the first official meeting in 1927. Encountering rather more than the usual long and stormy opposition and protests which seem to follow in the wake of any new innovation, it was not until the 1930s that the sport really got off the ground.

In 1769 Captain Cook sailed from England in the ship *Endeavour* on his voyage of discovery. It is on record that the famous naturalist Joseph Banks sailed with him taking two greyhounds, so perhaps these dogs running up and down the sands were the foundation of the great popularity of the greyhound in Australia today.

No dogs are allowed into Australia by air. As the quarantine period is shorter than that in England, by the time the greyhound has reached his destination, by sea, it is almost over. When a dog is travelling to Australia, the vetting and tests to ensure that he is entirely free from disease before he is allowed to embark are very stringent.

The two leading tracks in Australia are in Sydney, at Harold Park and Wentworth Park. Both tracks have a running surface of turf and it seems a unanimous world-wide opinion that the Australian turf, both on the greyhound and horse racing tracks, is the finest in the world. The two most important tracks in Victoria are Olympic Park and Sandown Park – but the running surfaces of these are of sand.

The facilities given to the Australian race-goer by the tracks do not compare with those of London's top tracks. The Totalisator Agency Board is the source of prize money in Australia and this must be the envy of English owners and trainers. The system in Australia is completely different from the English one. In England the tracks are owned by individuals and/or shareholders so the profits, less all the expenses, go to them.

Australia has the 'open kennel' system, as in Ireland, where all the greyhounds are owner-trained. (*See* OPEN KENNEL SYSTEM.) All moneys for the sport, including fees received from bookmakers, plus the profits from all other facilities given to patrons, and admission fees, go to the TAB. The TAB then ploughs back into the sport quite a large percentage of the profits, and this is one of the reasons why greyhound racing is thriving in Australia, perhaps more than in any other country. The metropolitan tracks are good, and these pay the most prize money. These tracks have anything from fifty to a hundred bookmakers betting at a meeting as, in Australia, bookmakers are only allowed to bet on the course.

TRACKS

Wentworth Park (The National Coursing Association Ltd, NSW): This beautiful Sydney racecourse – which has a turf-running surface – holds sixty meetings a year, in the evenings. Twenty-six of these are held on Saturdays and the remaining thirty-four on weekdays. Each meeting consists of ten eight-dog races, run over distances of 580 or 790 yards. The graded prize money is fantastic, compared with the English graded prize money. For a fifth-grade race at Wentworth Park, the greyhounds receive A$12,000 rising in a first-grade race to A$14,000.

The National Coursing Association Ltd introduced another feature event during 1973 to be run at this course. The Young Star Classic is for puppies of both sexes, up to two years of age, and the inaugural meeting is said to have revealed quite a number of up and coming champions.

Harold Park (NSW Greyhound Breeders, Owners and Trainers Association Ltd). This is the other top track in Sydney – run on similar lines to Wentworth Park – and also with sixty meetings a year, each of ten eight-dog races. Again, the running surface is of the finest turf and the distances of the races are either 500 or 800 yards. Prize money here is on the same generous scale, for graded and open races, as that of Wentworth Park.

Olympic Park, Melbourne: The winners and prize money for the Australian Cup (511 metres) held in Olympic Park for the years 1978 and 1979 were:

Australian Cup (1978): winner Count D'Argent, owned by Mrs C. Johnston and trained by Mr R. Johnston. Time of race: 30.19 secs. Prize money: A$25,000.

Australian Cup (1979): winner Boundless, owned and trained by Mrs J. Lew-Fatt. Time of race: 30.51 secs. Prize money: A$30,000.

RULES

Australian rules and regulations are similar to those of the National Greyhound Racing Club in England. The greyhounds have identification books but these, as in Ireland, are held by the owner of the greyhound. It is not such a simple matter – as it is in England – to acquire a complete record of the Australian dog's form, as the racing performances are not recorded on the Identity books as in England and Ireland.

PERSONALITIES

Some time ago, Frank K. Schock, a trainer in England, left with his wife and family to train in Australia, and I am greatly indebted to him for his information on Australian greyhound racing. He took with him the English greyhound, Which Chariot, purchased from the late George Flintham. This dog, a son of Cheerful Chariot out of Which Side, was trained when in England by Paddy Reilly of Walthamstow Stadium. In Australia, after breaking records on the race tracks, Which Chariot was retired to stud and, becoming Australia's leading sire, did more for breeding in that country than any other dog.

Also with trainer Frank Schock, at his Canberra kennels, are Ling Bird, who won England's Trafalgar Cup, the blue riband of the puppy races; Clifden Times who was favourite to win the English Derby outright, after his spectacular running in the semi-final; and Prince Champion (known as Prince's Imp when in England) a litter brother of Faithful Hope, winner of the English 1966 Derby. These dogs are standing at stud.

Gordon Hodson, one time trainer at the Greyhound Racing Association's White City Stadium, London, left in 1974 to train greyhounds in Australia. In 1979 he returned to England to train at the Brighton and Hove Stadium in Sussex.

One of his charges is a brindled greyhound dog, Playfield Royal, owned by HRH Prince Philip. This dog runs as hard as he can and, by winning races, is making considerable contributions to his owner's very worthy cause, The National Playing Fields Fund, for this is where his prize money goes.

Frank Schock tells me that although he occasionally hears of a snake being seen, he has seen none in Australia. Even in certain parts, where snakes are more abundant, it is very rare to hear that a person or animal has died from a bite.

The new greyhound track which opened at Cannington Central, near Perth, in December 1974, is said to be one of the finest in Australia. As is usual in Australia, through State legislation which allows no bookmakers to operate, all betting is through TAB (Totalisator Agency Board) with offices at the course and throughout Western Australia. The electronic Indicator Board and many other first-class facilities, including restaurants and car parks, are available to patrons.

Automatic Start: A device used on race-courses whereby the 'hare' releases the traps for opening as it passes by them.

Balanitis: Fortunately, something not well-known among greyhounds. It is an inflammation of the mucous membrane of the penis – causing purulent discharge from the prepuce. Most likely to be found among dogs used for stud, when growths may appear on the penis which are pink or red, irregular in shape, and bleed easily. The growths are contagious and a dog suffering from this complaint should not be used at stud.

Bitches are also liable to these growths and, until they are removed, and the bitch cured, she should not be used for breeding. If any suspicion of this complaint arises, your vet should be called.

Barm: (*see* BREAD). The froth or foam rising on fermented liquors; brewers yeast.

Barren: A bitch which is unable to produce puppies.

Bathing: A dog does not need, or like, a hot bath, so the temperature of the water should be either tepid or warm – 60°-80°F. If the water is hard, it is a good idea to add some Borax (obtainable from all chemists and druggists); this will soften the water and is soothing to the coat. There are very good medicated shampoos on the market, or a mild soap may be used. If the dog is dirty, or has fleas or any non-contagious skin trouble, there is a very good solution available in Britain called 'Kur-mange'. It is made by Cooper, McDougall and is very soothing. I have always found this obtainable at Boots chemists, if the branch has a department selling animal products. In powder form, it has to be mixed with a gallon of warm water. Do not rinse the coat, but squeeze out as much liquid as possible. Then take the dog for a gallop or run to help dry the coat. If the day is a cold one the dog should be rubbed hard with a dry towel on his return, but, in warmer weather, it should be left on for an hour or two and brushed out later.

Bedding: Modern conditions are a far cry from the days when we used to see a greyhound lying on a clean sweet-smelling bed of wheat straw. Much of the straw obtainable today could be the cause of skin trouble and coughing. It is often dusty and, what is even worse, contaminated with insecticide spray.

There have been several alternatives on the market such as shredded paper, but a lot of this proved non-absorbent. Ordinary newspaper is satisfactory although it looks rather 'poverty stricken'. It is clean, can be changed every day and fleas do not seem at all eager to settle on it. Thick newspaper spread on the floors keeps the kennel dry and is easily changed.

Benzole Benzoate: Obtained from chemists or druggists, this is useful for most forms of skin trouble. It should be diluted with a little water so that it is not too strong. The dog needs to be very carefully rubbed all over, so that the lotion penetrates the skin. If the weather is cold, it is better to do a part of the dog at a time – taking longer – since these applications for skin trouble are likely to have a chilling effect on the dog. Rub in, leave for three days, wash off in warm soapy water, and rinse. Repeat the treatment three times. Do not get the lotion in the dog's eyes.

Biliousness: Symptoms are usually the refusal of food, vomiting, thirst and, occasionally, diarrhoea. In bad cases the skin, eyes and mouth may turn yellowish.

A mild case is often put right by the dog himself when he may vomit to get rid of any excess bile, and will refuse food for up to twenty-four hours and then be perfectly all right again. If sickness, or a feeling of nausea, persists, he seems to have the sense to realize that he will be better without food for some hours. Water should be given, but it must be boiled first and then allowed to get cold.

First, give a dose (one tablespoonful) of castor oil. If the dog is inclined to take food, he should be given a light diet of invalid food. As in all cases of suspected illness, the temperature should be taken three times a day and, if this persists in staying at, or above, one and a half degrees above the normal of 101.5°F, then your vet should be called in.

Usually, in a case of biliousness, within twenty-four hours you will find your patient waiting for his food, wondering how you could ever have been so foolish as to think anything was wrong with him!

Bitches, Racing: No bitch is allowed to take part in a race or official trial, under NGRC rules, when in season, or until the veterinary surgeon passes her as fit to race. Stadiums will accept bitches into their kennels ten weeks after the first day of 'season'. A bitch's season date must be entered on the monthly 'Trainer's Return' sent to the NGRC offices, and it is then recorded on the Identity Book of the bitch. The date of season is also shown on the race card when the bitch is racing, as this knowledge can be useful to punters.

Bite: The adult greyhound has forty-two teeth. On the top jaw are twelve molars, two canine and six incisors. On the lower jaw are fourteen molars, two canine and six incisors.

Bites: A punctured wound caused by the bite of another animal. If the wound is deep it must be prevented from scabbing over without being properly treated, for this may result in an abscess forming. First, after cutting away the surrounding hair, cleanse the wound by syringing with a solution of warm water and boracic acid. This will prevent the wound from healing from the top. Amount to be used for wounds will be found on bottle of TCP obtainable from chemists and druggists. Boracic acid crystals from the same source should be 1 teaspoon of crystals to a tumbler of warm water. If the dog can reach the wound with his tongue he will treat the wound himself – with the healing properties in his saliva – by licking. When there is a serious wound your vet should be called in at once. (*See* ACCIDENTS.)

Bithel Bowls: The inventor of this feeding bowl, also the manufacturer, gave his name to it. He owned top-class racing dogs, the best-known being Model Dasher, a long-distance racer of the 1940s. He possibly knew that there isn't much a greyhound can't chew through when he sets his mind to it. The bowl is made of cast aluminium and is strong, clean and durable – and the only way to dispose of it is to lose it! No dog would be capable of chewing it. It is widely used in all greyhound kennels, stadium and otherwise, but I do not think it has the name Bithel on it these days.

Although at first it was exclusive to greyhounds, it is possibly used by large breeds of other dogs as well.

Fig. 1 Bithel bowl

These bowls are obtainable through the suppliers of greyhound equipment – names and addresses will be found in *The Greyhound Magazine* and the *Greyhound Owner*, under the advertisements.

Biting: Every dog is allowed to bite once before any action is taken. It is only after the dog has bitten twice that it may, in certain circumstances, have to be destroyed.

Bladder, Paralysis of: At first the dog is unable to pass water and, later, it just dribbles from him. Can be the result of an injury or strain, often of a stone in the bladder, or even the result of an over-clean dog being left too long in his kennel, when the bladder becomes over-distended, and this can be felt at the back of the abdomen.

A dog arrived in my kennels who had this trouble; it was the first I had seen of it. Although he went on to win many top-class open races whilst with me, he did have this trouble which sometimes recurred. I consulted Colonel Perry, FRCVS, vet to Wembley Stadium, and he gave me very good advice – which worked.

Treatment: Standing at the back of the dog, place a flat hand on either side of the abdomen, pressing the fingers in towards the hindquarters. This pressure on the walls of the abdomen gives the dog relief by the water gradually coming away. This I did several times a day when necessary, and I also found that a warm hot-water-bottle held on the abdomen for a short time helped. Barley water to drink also helps. If the dog passes no water for twenty-four hours, call your vet. There may a stone in the kidney, or it may be necessary to use a catheter.

Boarding Kennels: These are listed in *The Greyhound Magazine* which can be ordered from your newsagent, or direct from the Greyhound Magazine Co. Ltd, Bedford Chambers, Covent Garden, London WC2. Telephone: 01-836 8951. This magazine is issued monthly.

Bones: Raw marrow bones are extremely good for greyhounds to gnaw; they aid digestion and keep the teeth in order. A greyhound is expert in demolishing bones, and most butchers will supply these regularly, large enough to be gnawed but not swallowed. Once the dog has had a good session gnawing his bone, it should be removed. A bone to gnaw should never be given the day before racing or coursing, as quite a large amount of energy is used in gnawing, which is better saved for his race.

Raw bones are good for puppies too, especially when they are teething. A marrow bone cut into large enough sections, if possible with meat on (allowing one section for each puppy), will aid their digestion, help bring their teeth through without pain, and prevent them from supplementing their diet with stones. If possible, put the puppies separately with their bones, otherwise a referee will be needed.

Cooked bones are very dangerous when given to dogs. At the very least they cause constipation, which may be distressing. Game bones are dangerous. We know that foxes eat them and so would dogs in their wild state, but it would then be with the flesh and roughage, feathers, etc., which would give a degree of protection and, again, they would be raw. Many vets agree that the cooked chop and cutlet bones are high on the danger list and can give the dog great pain when swallowed and could cause choking and fatal damage to the inside. (*See* CHOKING.)

Box Muzzles: (*see* Fig. 2) Sometimes, when dogs have any medication on them which should not be licked, it is necessary that a leather box muzzle should be worn. There should be two in use, one on and one being dried, otherwise the muzzle after frequent use can become moist and soggy and may make the mouth sore. In hot weather, it is better to use a wire racing muzzle, covered with muslin or cotton net. This will serve the same purpose, and be much cooler.

As an extra safeguard it can also be worn when a dog is put in a kennel to await his race.

Bread: The ideal bread, especially for training purposes, can easily be made at home. Use three parts of first grade wholemeal flour and one

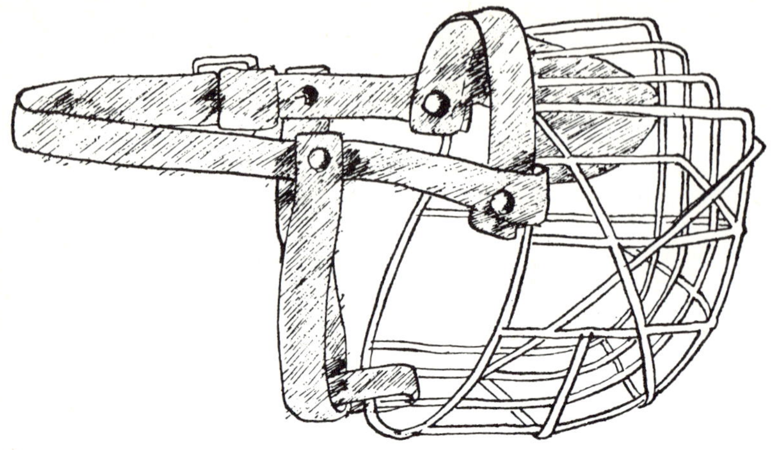

Fig. 2 Box muzzle

part oatmeal (the oatmeal may be left out in summer as it is rather heating). Biscuits made from the same ingredients, in the same proportion, make a welcome change.

From *The Greyhound*, by 'Stonehenge', 1853: 'To make brown bread without barm [c.f.]. Take of flour 12 pounds; bicarbonate of soda two ounces; mix them well together with the hands or by sifting through a fine sieve; then mix two ounces of muriatic acid with eight pints of water, stirring it well with an earthenware or glass rod; afterwards stir the acid and water quickly into the flour, using the same rod or a wooden spoon for the purpose.'

The dough should then be quickly put into common earthenware flower pots, filling them about two-thirds full, and baked immediately in a quick oven, rather hotter than for common bread. In this method there is no loss or change by fermentation, and the acid and soda combine to form common salt, so that there is nothing pernicious to the dog, and yet the bread is light enough to soak well.

It has an agreeable natural taste, and keeps moist and good for ten days, if in an airy place; it is also easily prepared, not taking more than a quarter of an hour from the commencement to the putting into the oven. There is also a saving of ten per cent in the weight. In the common process the saccharine part of the flour, with a portion of the gum and the gluten, is lost by being converted into carbonic acid gas and spirit which are driven into the air by heat, and this waste is incurred solely to obtain carbonic acid gas to raise the dough. In the soda and acid process the gas is obtained in a much more simple way, without loss and without decomposition of the nutritive materials existing in the flour.

Wheat and oatmeal may be mixed in any proportion which may agree best with the dogs, and which varies a good deal in different districts, according to climate, soil, and warmth. (*See* MURIATIC ACID.)

Breath, Bad: This is often due to bad teeth, especially in an old dog. If these are causing pain or distress it is advisable to consult your vet. Teeth can easily be removed painlessly under an anaesthetic. The presence of worms in the body will also cause bad breath, which will disappear when the parasites are removed. Normally, well-cared for and well-groomed dogs have no odour if they have access to fresh grass.

Breech Birth: When a puppy at birth arrives at the vulva feet first, instead of the normal position of head first. This can be serious with breeds with large heads but the slim-headed greyhound should present no danger.

Breeder: Is the legal owner or lessee of the dam at the time of whelping. It is essential that the dam is registered with the Kennel Club, for show purposes, and the National Coursing Club for racing or coursing. When a dam is leased from the owner on breeding terms, a letter of agreement must be produced for either Club for registration of the puppies.

Britain's Greyhound Trainer of the Year 1978: This award was won by Geoffrey DeMulder of Coventry, who was selected by members of the Greyhound Trainers' Association and the Breeders' Forum to receive this award. The winner's father, was part owner and trainer of the 1974 English Derby winner, Jimsun – pictured with Geoffrey's daughter, Ruth (*see* photograph section).

Broadcasting (BBC Local Radio): An interesting and useful programme of greyhound racing news, comments and selections, is broadcast from London Broadcasting.

Tune in to Mike Palmer (of the *Sporting Life*) each weekday evening at 5.50 pm and Saturday mornings at 7.15 and 8.15 am. All the latest information on greyhound racing on 261 MW and 97.3 VHF.

Listen to greyhound news from the BBC's 20 Local Radio Stations: Birmingham – Blackburn – Brighton – Bristol – Carlisle – Derby – Humberside – Leeds – Leicester – London – Manchester – Medway – Merseyside – Newcastle – Nottingham – Oxford – Sheffield – Solent – Stoke and Teeside.

Broken Bones: (*see* FRACTURES).

Bronchitis: (Acute) Catarrhal inflammation of the larger bronchial tubes.

Causes: Often after or during distemper or through exposure to cold and wet, draughts, or infection. Becoming chilled after hard exercise, or living in hot stuffy rooms or damp, badly ventilated kennels are other causes.

Symptoms: A rise in temperature, when shivering may also occur, and the patient is dull and listless. A cough, which may be slight at first but then more severe and frequent, and the breathing may be difficult. A dog that is fed correctly and has plenty of exercise, or liberty, is not so susceptible to bronchial troubles.

As soon as bronchitis is suspected the dog should be isolated in a warm, well-ventilated kennel or room, and he should wear a rug or body-jacket, or jumper. When breathing is difficult, and the throat seems congested with phlegm, give an emetic (piece of soda twice the size of a hazel-nut). Two or three times a day he should inhale. The usual long-spouted kettle used for human beings can be used but, as this has to be kept over heat, it can be dangerous. Improvise with a bowl filled with boiling water (or at least hot enough to give off plenty of steam) to which has been added a solution of Friar's Balsam and Menthol which your chemist or druggist will make up for you. Either hold the dog near enough to the bowl to inhale the fumes or put a cloth over your head and his, being careful to keep him firm so that he cannot injure himself by getting in the hot water.

Bronchitis: (Chronic) This is when the inflammation reaches the smaller bronchial tubes, and is a much more serious disease. It can be a complication of a disease of the lung. The same treatment will be as for acute bronchitis, but the jacket or jumper may be lined with Thermogene (from chemists or druggists) in the region of the chest and lungs.

Brood Bitch, Choice of: It is important to breed from the best available bitch. Buy or lease a bitch of the right blood, mate her to the right dog, and you cannot go far wrong. It is well to remember that her puppies are more likely to inherit the general characteristics of her family, rather than the individual points she herself possesses. See that she comes from proved racing or coursing stock. Many greyhounds bred today are not interested in chasing anything, because they are not jealous enough. (*See* JEALOUSY.)

A greyhound is not eligible to race under National Greyhound Racing Club rules until it is fifteen months old. Then, if she is racing for three or four seasons, a bitch may be five years old before having her first litter. This is no problem, since parturition is easier in the greyhound

1. The Show Greyhound. Ch. Royser Poner, Best of Breed at Cruft's 1970, owned by Mr R. Parsons (*By permission of the owner*)

2. The Racing Greyhound. Sherry's Prince, the open-race hurdles champion and winner of seventy-one races including three English Grand Nationals. Owned by Mrs Joyce Matthews (*By permission of the owner*)

3. Jimsun, the 1974 English Derby winner, owned by Mr J. DeMulder and Miss L. Walker. Here with Ruth, daughter of the dog's trainer Geoffrey DeMulder, son of the part-owner (*By permission of the owner*)

4. (*below*): Patricia's Hope, the 1972 and 1973 English Derby winner (*By permission of the Greyhound Racing Association*)

than in any other breed of dog, as whelps are small in comparison with the size of the dam. Whelping troubles are therefore very few and far between.

Brood Bitch, Feeding: Even if the bitch has been used to only one meal a day, she should be given two after mating. A light morning feed between 7 and 8 am, and an afternoon meal between 4 and 5 pm, which should be the main meal of the day.

These feeds may consist of:

Morning: Half a pint of goat's or cow's milk, with one teaspoonful of honey, or Virol, or glucose, with one *new laid* unbeaten raw egg, and rusk or stale wholemeal bread. Rusk may be substituted, for a change, with Shredded Wheat, or similar breakfast cereals.

Afternoon: 1 lb of raw meat, cut up but not minced, with rusk or stale wholemeal bread and gravy on three afternoons of the week. Horsemeat is best fed raw, grilled or roasted as when boiled a great deal of the goodness will go into the gravy – which is unsuitable for dogs and one of the causes of some skin troubles. (*See* FEEDING.)

Substitutes for the other afternoons of the week may be cooked beef, tripe, sheeps' paunches, sheeps' head, fish, etc. These foods are all nourishing – but slightly more weight of tripe or fish should be given. The gravy from any of these foods may be added to the rusk or meal together with cooked onions or garlic. A little chopped watercress, or chopped cabbage stump may also be added to the feed but, apart from this cooked vegetables are not recommended. A little scraped raw carrot may be added to a meal.

After four to five weeks from the day of mating the bitch will need extra meat, and this should be gradually increased possibly up to 2 lb per day; also a liberal allowance of milk. It will now be better to give her three meals a day, rather than too large a meal at one time. It is better for the bitch to receive the vitamins she needs, and which are so necessary at this time, through the natural foods she is given, rather than by any direct doses of vitamins. Her own body will provide a great deal of calcium, vital at this time for the growth and well-being of the coming puppies, and one source of supply will be through the fresh milk she is given. Give goat's milk if available or otherwise cow's milk; this she will appreciate before going to bed.

Brood Bitch, Management of: With the present rule that a puppy's age is taken from the first day of the month in which it is born (*see* AGE FOR RACING), the best time to mate the bitch is from early January. This will ensure that puppies come straight from the nest into the better weather, which should give longer days and hours of sunlight. Added to which, there is no need for any artificial heating; and all young things grow better and sturdier with some sun on their backs.

The time to put the bitch to the sire is from the tenth day of heat but, if you are certain when the first day of heat commenced, then about the sixteenth day is the best time. When booking the mating to the sire, it is best to ask advice from the stud groom, or owner in charge of the dog.

After mating, the bitch should be kept away from molestation by other dogs until all signs of heat have vanished – at least until the thirtieth day from the first day of heat. During this time the bitch should be allowed in a safe paddock for exercise, and also taken for walks.

Bitches in whelp are best without a lot of medicine but, three weeks after service, the bitch should be wormed. Your vet can supply the necessary dose, but there are many safe and effective worm remedies obtainable from chemists or druggists. The instructions should be closely followed and, as with all medicines, the dose given should never be larger than stated.

After thirty days from the first day of her season the bitch may go back with a dog, or a bitch she has been used to living with, and may lead a normal life for seven weeks after mating. Then she should be taken from the other dog and allowed to wander as she likes in her own paddock – preferably the paddock where she will have her puppies. She will very much appreciate human company at this time and should still be taken for walks – but these should be slowed down a little if she is heavy in whelp.

At night the bitch should sleep in the whelping shed, but should be let out into her paddock last thing. Then she should be given a drink of milk with the chill taken off, mixed with a teaspoonful of honey or Virol, and two slices of wholemeal or Hovis rusk. Give the rusk separately, and she will possibly take this back to bed with her when, if necessary, she should be shut in for the night. The rusk will help to keep her teeth in good condition, as it is not safe to give her bones.

It is important that the bitch is absolutely clean at the time of parturition and, a day or two before the puppies are due, her breasts and stomach and the surrounding parts under her tail should be wiped with a clean soft cloth, first wrung out in warm water. Then dry her gently with a towel. Despite all we do, worms seem to be present in newborn puppies, but this may help: two or three days before the puppies' arrival, give the bitch one dessertspoonful of medicinal paraffin, in some warm milk last thing at night, and repeat the next night. Do not give any strong laxative.

Usually, bitches have their puppies on the sixty-second or sixty-third day, counting the day of mating. Sometimes a large litter arrives earlier and a small litter may come later – but puppies seldom live if born before the fifty-seventh day (*see* WHELPING).

Buttermilk: This is good for puppies and older dogs alike; in the summer there is nothing better for the blood.

Calculated Time: An assessment of race times of all runners is taken from the winner's recorded actual time. Allowances are then taken, or added, for the 'going' – the state of the track. If the track is considered 'normal' the time stands as it is.

Basic time calculations: Short Head (0.01 sec); Head (0.02 sec); Neck (0.03 sec); ½ length (0.04 sec); ¾ length (0.06 sec); 1 length (0.08 sec). One length = 1 metre.

Cancer: A progressive, malignant tumour, which destroys the tissues of the part in which it grows. If diagnosed at an early stage, an operation may be successful, so consult your vet immediately if any swelling or lump which cannot be accounted for is noticed on the dog. With a slow-growing tumour, malignant or non-malignant, the dog's temperature is unlikely to rise as it would in the case of an abscess (*see* ABSCESS and TUMOUR).

Carroll's International Owners' Invitation Stakes: An international race, between American, British and Irish owned greyhounds, was long looked forward to in the racing world – and this competition took place in September 1974. This may prove to be the only race of its kind unless quarantine rules are waived for American entries – and this is not likely.

It wasn't considered practical to bring American dogs here, nor to Ireland, because of the rigid quarantine laws which apply to animals entering either country. This would have meant strict confinement for the American dogs for six months – and further time to get them back into racing condition. There are no quarantine laws between Britain and Ireland.

This was overcome by Mr Aaron Kulchinsky coming from America to Ireland and purchasing six dogs so that they could then compete, in his ownership. The competition was run on a points basis with three National Heats run at Dublin's Shelbourne Park Stadium on 9 September; one heat for the greyhounds in American ownership; one heat for those in British ownership and another for those in Irish ownership. The winner and second in each of these heats went forward to the Major Final run at Shelbourne Park on 14 September. The third and fourth in the Shelbourne heats went into a second final – or consolation race – also run at Shelbourne Park on 14 September. The teams then went to the White City Stadium, London, and completed the competition here on 24 and 28 September.

Major Final Run at Shelbourne Park Stadium, Dublin on 14 September 1974.
1st Tommy Astaire (USA)
2nd Monalee Expert (IRE)
3rd Two P.M. (GB)
4th Carrowkeal Ref (GB)
5th Waverley Supreme (IRE)
6th Bowler Flash (USA)
Won by 4 l. 550 flat Time 30.35 (track record)
Tommy Astaire (Bd [brindled] dog February 1972). Sire: Ivy Hall Flash – Dam: Miami Star II. Owned and trained by A. Kulchinsky, USA

Major Final Run at White City Stadium, London on 28 September 1974.
1st Carrowkeal Ref (GB)
2nd Bowler Flash (USA)
3rd Lady Devine (IRE)
4th Silent Thought (IRE)
5th Two P.M. (GB)
6th More Silver (USA)
Won by 3 l. 550 flat Time 30.09
Carrowkeal Ref (Be [blue] dog July 1972. Sire: Kilberg Kuda – Dam: Rye Queen.
Winners: Ireland 32 points, GB 27 points, USA 25 points.

Caroll's 525 International, 1980: The first prize of £3,500 was won by Jelly Crock in a time of 29.80 secs for the Dundalk course. Second was Hurry on Bran and third prize was won by Flying Marble.

Castration: The neutering of a male greyhound (*see* SPAYING, for the bitch). This is very rare in greyhounds and has no advantage as regards coursing or racing. A castrated greyhound would be allowed to race, except in the classic races where it would not be accepted as an entry. Quite unacceptable in the show ring.

Championship Shows: Open Shows under club rules at which Challenge Certificates are competed for.

Charcoal (activated): Charcoal tablets, obtainable from your chemist or druggist, will absorb poisons and are useful in the case of stomach upset or diarrhoea. Give two or three tablets every eight hours. It is also beneficial to give two tablets to a racing greyhound two nights before a race and he will willingly take them with his food.

Choice of Sire: (*see* BROOD BITCH, CHOICE OF).

Choking: Dogs can choke themselves when eating bones, especially chop or cutlet bones and also sometimes with a large piece of meat which becomes lodged in the gullet. This is not too serious as, if it cannot be pulled up, it is usually possible to push it down with the fingers. When a bone or other obstacle becomes lodged in the back of the throat the dog coughs and retches violently. Usually, the bone passes down the gullet but as it reaches the place where the gullet narrows, is usually prevented from going further which causes the dog very great distress. He keeps gulping as if trying to swallow. A few pieces of meat given to him may force the bone on but, if the bone remains stationary, he will reject or vomit all solid food. He may be able to swallow beef-tea, eggs and milk, etc.

Your veterinary surgeon may be able to help by using forceps – or an operation may be necessary – if the dog has survived to go through this painful treatment. (*See* BONES.)

Chlorophyl: Chlorophyl is the green colouring matter found in plants, especially in grasses, stinging nettles and bramble bushes. Dogs kept in a house or kennel, even when regularly groomed and bathed, may have a 'doggy' smell. All dogs will readily eat and enjoy fresh grass; working greyhounds, knowing free gallops and large grassy paddocks, very seldom can be accused of having a doggy smell.

Chromatography: The pre-race testing which is undertaken at a large number of National Greyhound Racing Club's racecourses involves the taking of urine samples from the greyhounds which are due to race, approximately ninety minutes before the first race, and before the greyhounds are placed in their racing kennels. These samples are taken to the pre-race testing laboratories, which are generally sited adjacent to the racing kennels, where staff trained in the techniques evolved by Glasgow University carry out tests in respect of the following groups of drugs: (a) Barbiturates; (b) Alkaloids; (c) Chlorals. The Chromatography system is used in detecting whether any drugs have been administered in regard to the Barbiturate and Alkaloid groups, and a separate test is made in relation to the Chloral group.

These tests generally take one hour to conclude, so it is possible for a racecourse management to know before a race whether any greyhound has been given any drug – whether under the jurisdiction of a veterinary surgeon or otherwise. The use of these units means that the public has a very great additional safeguard, and they know the greyhounds are running to the best of their natural ability.

In the event of any sample proving positive, the local Steward will, after consultation with the veterinary surgeon, consider the withdrawal of that greyhound. Glasgow University provides the detailed analytical process that is required before any disciplinary action is taken against the owner, or trainer, of the greyhound concerned.

The NGRC have undertaken a considerable research programme with Glasgow University, together with Instaprint Camera Company, who operate the units commercially on licence from the NGRC.

Strong security measures can be put into action. A strong linkwire enclosure can be built round the kennels, with an installed underground wiring system, operated by hidden batteries. When set to 'on', this will trigger off alarms in the house if any kennel door is opened in the range. Flood-lighting can also be operated from inside the house. Whatever system is used to help guard these dogs, a fulltime watch is still necessary.

There is no doubt that the chromatography tests, and anything similar, are a vital necessity to ensure the survival of racing. The inexplicable running of a genuine greyhound will cause falling attendances at tracks, for so many people know that a greyhound, if fit, and if he has once shown that he likes the game, will give of his best at all times. He doesn't know the difference between running in a graded race or the final of the Derby.

With a drive to protect racing animals, as ways and means improve in detecting substances and drugs which may be fed to them, it may be even more vital than ever to detect simple practices which leave no obvious trace, such as interference with the most vital point – the eyes. Without clear sight no animal can safely race at speed (*see* DRUGS).

Chorea (or St Vitus's Dance): Usually a result of distemper or hard pad when the nervous system has been impaired. A twitching in almost any part of the body which, although it may lessen with time, is usually incurable.

Circumcision: (*see* SHEATH). A small surgical operation necessary when the sheath covering the penis will not easily allow this to retract after mating.

Coats and Rugs: Well-fed and well-cared for greyhounds do not normally need coating, or rugging as it is often called, when walking or at exercise.

Whilst it is not wise to coddle these dogs, it must be remembered that they haven't the dense coats of many other canines; so rugs are sometimes needed. These can be obtained from H. J. Porter (Greyhounds) Ltd, Hendon, London, or from suppliers who advertise in *The Greyhound Magazine* and *The Greyhound Owner*.

There is the rug with the hood for day wear, and the one without a hood (which simply means that it does not come up so high at the neck). This coat is better for night wear, or in sickness, as it is fastened with strings instead of a buckle. Coats are needed in very cold weather for travelling, after strenuous exercise and when the dog is standing around in cold and windy weather. This is very important when at a stadium kennel waiting for routine kennelling. As greyhounds have even less fur under the belly than on their backs, it is advisable to put a small woolly jumper underneath the rug in cold weather (*see* NURSING). This helps to keep the wind and cold from all quarters, and is very useful in the racing kennel, where the dog often has to spend a long time before his race. String vests can also be used.

Cod Liver Oil: This is very rich in Vitamin A and is beneficial in the treatment of rickets, debility, etc., but should be used sparingly.

Colic: Mostly affects puppies who have eaten rubbish. It may also affect adult dogs, especially after too strong a medicine being given for worms. The dog will be restless and, if the pain is very severe, may cry and howl. There may also be vomiting and diarrhoea.

Treatment: If there is no diarrhoea a dose of castor oil may put this right, but if there is any rising of temperature, your vet should be called.

Colitis: Inflammation of the colon (large intestine). (*See* COLIC.)

Collapse: The dog lies in a semi-conscious state, and his eyes are glassy looking. The condition may arise from shock, such as after an accident, or haemorrhage. In the latter case, the gums and inside of cheeks and eyelids will be very pale.

Let the dog lie very quietly on his *right* side. If the body is cold, put hot-water bottles round it; these should be wrapped in cloths so that they do not burn the dog.

One of the symptoms of internal haemorrhage (say after a dog has been run over) is that the stomach will feel very cold. Do not move the dog, for any reason, whilst he is still unconscious.

If possible, telephone your vet, for the dog may need stimulants before the vet can reach you. The most likely to be at hand would be coffee or brandy. Give enema of strong black coffee or, alternatively, fifteen drops of brandy in warm milk; blood heat 100-101°F. (*See* ENEMA.)

Collars and Leads: For safety's sake, the leather fish-tail collar, and long leather lead with buckle each end, should always be used when a greyhound is being led or exercised. The collar will not restrict the dog's breathing and, if properly adjusted, he cannot slip from this. The lead, safely buckled at each end, has no stitching to become loose. If the greyhound should escape and run free with the lead and collar on, the lead will trail behind him and be unlikely to catch in his feet, causing injury.

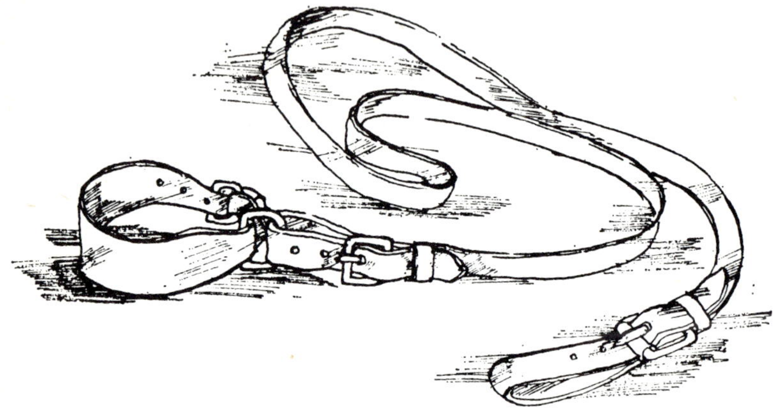

Fig. 3 Collar and lead

Colostrum: This is in the first milk the bitch gives to her puppies after whelping and acts as an immuniser against disease until they are old enough to receive proper injections. It is one of the most important factors in the puppy's early life and is irreplaceable in artificial milk.

Colour: This does not seem to count for much in the greyhound world, where it is said that a good dog cannot be a bad colour, but, at least towards racing and coursing greyhounds, there has always been a strong aversion to 'blues'. They are reputed to lack determination but this is possibly because the blue dog, almost without exception, has light eyes. This is a great handicap at speed, as the light eye is weaker and has not the strong, quick sight of the darker eye.

Many years ago, white whelps were always destroyed at birth, being considered very unlucky. This may have originated with the arrival of King Canute. When this Danish king arrived to become King of England (1017-66) he decreed that only Royalty and 'people of quality' were to own greyhounds. If found in other ownership, the dogs were so badly mutilated about the legs that they could neither run nor walk.

Colour of greyhounds for registration: The recognized standard colours of greyhounds are black, blue, brindled, red, fawn and ticked (light flecks on dark or dark flecks on light colours). Abbreviations of colours that appear in race cards are: bk; be; bd; r; f; w and tkd. Where there is a combination of colours, the predominant colour is put first. Colours of young puppies (under eight weeks), when registered with the National Coursing Club as a litter, are allowed to be altered within six months from date of birth, if these have changed slightly as they sometimes do.

Constipation: *Symptoms:* the motions are hard, dry, large and difficult to pass. The dog instead of having an action at least once a day, may have one only every two or three days.

Treatment: A great deal can be done by diet. In ordinary cases, give the dog gentle exercise and carefully regulate the food. Rusk soaked in some soup, mixed with meat and some green vegetable added makes a good principal meal. For a second or evening meal the rusk may be given dry. For a change of diet give some raw liver, which is very good as a laxative, apart from being nourishing. In obstinate cases a laxative may be given, such as one tablespoonful of Dinneford's fluid magnesia, each morning in a little milk. In some cases, salad oil answers best and, for the adult greyhound, one dessertspoonful should be given daily for a fortnight. (*See* ENEMA.)

Contract Training: Large tracts of land in England are today fetching vast sums of money for building and development purposes. With the rising costs of transport and maintenance of the large establishments necessary for the kennelling and training of greyhounds, many stadiums are now selling the properties providing these facilities. As an alternative, they are reverting to 'contract training' (as in the United States).

This is a system whereby a trainer is contracted to a stadium to keep and train greyhounds in his own kennels – and to present them for the races at that stadium. Expenses for transport, etc., are arranged, and there is increased prize money for racing. The National Greyhound Racing Club have always granted licences to private trainers (renewable each year) provided the applicants and the conditions of kennelling and training were approved. This was only for greyhounds to compete in 'open' races.

Now a contract trainer will be able to keep all grades of dogs to race at the stadium to which he is contracted and, as always, take his charges to any NGRC track for open racing.

Convulsions in Puppies: These sometimes occur when a puppy is infested with worms or when the second teeth are coming through. Although the puppy has seemed quite well, he may suddenly tumble over, kicking his legs and champing his jaws. The puppy should be held so that he doesn't hurt himself by running about. Keep the puppy quiet for a time in a dark, cool room. Feed on a milk diet for a few days and, to prevent a recurrence, treat for worms.

Copulation: If ready for mating, the bitch on being presented to the dog will raise her tail and will stand firmly, giving every indication of willingness. When the dog is repulsed, a period of play in a paddock together will sometimes have the desired effect but, if not, the bitch must be taken away and presented the next day.

During the mating, they should become 'tied' or 'locked' together; this is caused by a swelling at the base of the male organ which prevents his withdrawal for a time. The dog will usually dismount, after service, and prop his hind-leg over the back of the bitch when they will remain tied hind-quarter to hind-quarter, and this is the natural position for them to adopt until they are able to break free naturally. Great care must be taken to see that the stud is not subjected to undue strain by the bitch trying to break free. Apart from not wishing any animal to suffer unnecessary injury, top stud dogs and bitches are very valuable and it is advisable to have two people to assist at the mating.

After mating the bitch should be put back into her kennel to rest. The dog, after mating, should also be put back in his kennel, as soon as his penis has retracted into the sheath. (*See* VAGINA, INJURIES TO.)

Corrugated Iron: This should never be used in any kennels or buildings housing dogs. It is hot in summer and cold in winter, and causes condensation.

Coughing: The cough, apart from that present in distemper, is more often than not a symptom of worms, and after the removal of the worms the cough will disappear.

Dusty straw or bedding will also cause coughing in some dogs, the straw being much more likely to do so these days as a result of combine harvesting and the extensive use of insecticides. (*See* VOMITING.)

Coursing: King James I of England (1566-1625) is reputed to have made coursing a very popular pursuit in England. In 1776 the famous Swaffham Club was founded by Lord Orford – also famous for his experimental breeding with greyhounds. At this time his friend, the Duke of Norfolk, laid down a set of rules for coursing one of which was: No hare to be coursed with more than a brace of greyhounds.

Today the National Coursing Club, in London, is the governing body of all authorized coursing in England. As keepers of the *Greyhound Stud Book*, they are also responsible for all initial registrations of greyhounds wishing to race under National Greyhound Racing Club rules.

The blue riband of coursing is the Waterloo Cup – run in February each year at Altcar. Since its inception in 1836, the greatest coursing dog is considered to have been Fullerton, winner of the Waterloo Cup in four successive years (1889-92). However, according to records, it seems that many judges were of the opinion that Master M'Grath, a three times winner of the cup, had no equal for pace, cleverness and killing power. This dog, in his fourth season, won the Brownlow Cup at Lurgan in October 1870 and, in the following year, won his third Waterloo Cup – winning eleven courses without losing one. Master M'Grath, was a very small dog (52-54 lb) and it is interesting to note how much smaller the dogs were in those days than they are now. Many of the winners were below 60 lb in weight, although the 1859 winner (Selby) is recorded as having weighed 75 lb. There is always controversy in comparing something from a previous generation with its present-day counterpart, and one needs to be brave to do so; but if we are to believe that some of these greyhounds walked as far as one hundred miles to the coursing ground (though not in one day), surely, the energy of some must have been expended and left some of the competitors 'more equal than others'.

There is no doubt that the speed of the coursing greyhound has greatly improved since the nineteenth and early twentieth centuries but they now course much stronger hares. Hares which were then reported as having weighed 5 lb would scale another 3 or 4 lb today, due to the intensive cultivation of the land, which gives them access to much better feed. Top racing greyhounds are seldom seen coursing, perhaps because the training is entirely different. The racing dog requires neither the working abilities, nor the terrific staying power of the coursing dog. However, Mr H. E. Gocher's famous racing greyhound, Endless Gossip, winner of the English Derby and the Scottish Derby, in 1952 then went on to run brilliantly in the Waterloo Cup and, had he not been so hard-run in the fourth round, might easily have won the trophy.

Extract from the NATIONAL COURSING CLUB'S BOOK OF RULES

Illegal Practices

1 The Club will not under any circumstances countenance any of the following practices, namely:

(a) The use of ground for coursing into which hares have been artificially moved or transported during the previous six months.

(b) The use of ground for coursing where the hares have not been at liberty for the previous six months.

(c) The use of ground for coursing which in the opinion of the Standing Committee is designed to restrict artificially the complete freedom and liberty of the hares.

2 The Standing Committee may, if upon due enquiry it finds that any affiliated Club has been guilty of the foregoing practices, order that such Club be expelled from affiliation and disqualified from becoming affiliated for five years.

Organization of Coursing Meetings

1 For any proposed Coursing Meeting a Committee of not less than three shall be formed, who shall appoint a Meeting Secretary and with him settle the preliminaries.

2 The Committee and Meeting Secretary may appoint the Judge and Slipper, in which case their names shall be announced simultaneously with the announcement of the Coursing Meeting and notified to the Secretary.

3 The Committee of the Coursing Meeting shall elect Stewards, who shall be Coursers of repute who have signified their intention of being present at the Coursing Meeting. The number of Stewards to be elected shall be three or five unless the Meeting Secretary is a Steward *ex officio,* when the number to be elected shall be four. The management of the Coursing Meeting shall be in the hands of the Committee and Stewards.

The Stewards shall have full control over Judge, Slipper, Slip Steward and Flag Steward, and those in charge of dogs. They shall have power to suspend any of these persons, such suspension not to extend beyond the Coursing Meeting and to be immediately reported to the Standing Committee. The Meeting Secretary shall:

Have in his possession at the Coursing Meeting an up-to-date copy of the Bye-Laws and Code of Rules and a copy of the current edition of the *Stud Book.*

Slip Steward

The duties of a Slip Steward shall be:

(a) To see that the right dogs, both in courses and byes, are brought to slips in their proper turn, at the right time and wearing the right collars.

(b) To report to the Stewards without delay any dog that does not come to the slips correctly, and any act on the part of the Slipper, a nominator, or his representatives which the Slip Steward considers should be brought to their knowledge.

Taking Dogs to the Slips

Every dog brought to the slips shall wear a collar not less than 2 inches wide and coloured red for the dog on the left hand side of the slips (collar usually knitted of wool).

No allowance shall be made for any mistake, but if the wrong dogs have run together in any round, and the mistake is not discovered until another round has been run, no objection can be made, and the course must stand as run.

The Slip

The order to slip may be given either by the Judge or the Slip Steward, or the Stewards may leave the slip to the sole discretion of the Slipper. The length of the slip must necessarily vary with the nature of the ground, and where practicable should not be less than four score yards.

Decision of the Judge

The Judge shall be subject to any general rules which may be established by the Club for his guidance.

He shall, on the termination of each course, immediately deliver his decision, either by displaying a red or white handkerchief corresponding to the collar on the winner or, when the colours of the dogs are more easily distinguishable than their collars, he may call the colour of the winning dog aloud.

He shall not recall or reverse his decision, on any pretext whatever, after it has been declared; but no decision shall be delivered until the Judge is perfectly satisfied that the course is absolutely terminated.

Principles of Judging

The Judge shall decide all courses upon the one uniform principle that the dog which scores the greater number of points during the continuance of the course is to be declared the winner. The principle is to be carried out by estimating the value of the work done by each dog, as seen by the Judge, upon a balance of points according to the scale hereafter laid down, from which also are to be deducted certain specified allowances and penalties.

Points of the Course

(a) Speed, which shall be estimated as one, two or three points, according to the degree of superiority shown.

(b) The Go-Bye – two points, or if gained on the outer circle, three points.

(c) The Turn – one point.

(d) The Wrench – half a point.

(e) The Kill. Not more than one point, in proportion to the degree of merit displayed in that kill, which may be of no value.

(f) The Trip – one point.

Under no circumstance is speed without subsequent work to be allowed to decide a course except where great superiority is shown by one dog over another in a long lead to covert. If a dog after gaining the first six points, still keeps possession of the hare by superior speed, he shall have double the prescribed allowance for the subsequent points made before his opponent begins to score.

The Go-Bye is where a dog starts a clear length behind his opponent and yet passes him in a straight run, and gets a clear length before him.

The Turn is where the hare is brought round at not less than a right angle from her previous line.

The Wrench is where the hare is bent from her line at less than a right angle; but where she only leaves her line to suit herself, and not from the dog pressing her, nothing is to be allowed.

The Merit of a Kill must be estimated according to whether a dog by his own superior dash and skill, bears the hare, whether he picks her up through any little accidental circumstances favouring him, or whether she is turned into his mouth by the other dog.

Coursing Clubs in England: run under National Coursing Club rules.

Alresford:	Sutton Scotney, Hampshire.
Altcar:	Near Liverpool. Extensive grounds where England's Waterloo Cup is run.
Colchester:	Near Acton Sudbury.
Coquetdale and Border:	Near Swindon.
Durham County:	Near Durham.
East of England:	Near Spalding.
Huntingdon:	Near Huntingdon.
Isle of Ely:	Near Bottisham, Cambridgeshire.
Isle of Wight:	Isle of Wight.
Kimberley and Wymondham:	Near Kimberley.
Mid-Essex:	Near Harlow.
North Herts:	Near Weston.
North Lincs:	Near Horncastle.
Oxfordshire:	Near Blenheim.

Scottish National:	Near Annan.
Sherburn Farmers:	Near Malton.
South of England:	Near Newmarket.
Swaffham:	Near Hockwald, Norfolk.
United Coursing:	Near Huntingdon.
Whittlesey and March:	Near Whittlesey, Cambridgeshire.
Yeovil and Sherborne:	King Weston, Somerset.
Old Yorkshire:	Near Thirsk.

Coursing, Guide to: *A Brief Guide to Coursing Run Under National Coursing Club Rules* is available, free of charge, from the National Coursing Club, 35/37 Grosvenor Gardens, London SW1.

Coursing, Pros and Cons: There is a great deal of controversy over the practice of coursing and a few facts are given below.

People do, quite rightly, think that the killing of a defenceless animal is cruel. Man in the main *is* cruel for the simple reason that he has brain enough always to provide a very good excuse as to why he should do something he wants to, irrespective of the outcome.

Had I not moved to the country early in 1939, I might possibly now be saying, like many others, that all blood sports should be stopped. However, I *have* lived in the country and have seen some of the appalling alternatives provided by man. Nature is itself cruel, for I cannot think of any wild animal on earth which hasn't another to prey upon it; perhaps because nature's only real law is the survival of the fittest, which animals seem to accept. It is man, with the unnecessary prolonging of the death of an animal which has to be killed, who is wrong.

Coursing the Dummy Hare: Live coursing continues in many countries, but there is a great deal of controversy as to its future.

A greyhound experienced in coursing, in Britain, does not often chase the racing 'dummy' with the same determination he shows towards the live quarry. Many owners of the top racing greyhounds are reluctant to try them on the coursing field as, apart from any other reason, there is the risk of the dogs being over-run should other hares be turned up before the contestants have been caught after running courses.

This does not apply to Ireland, where most greyhounds go coursing before, between and after their track commitments. Here the system is park coursing where the area is confined and prevents the dogs from being over-run.

Once again, America is first in the field to offer an alternative to live coursing, through the Lure Tronic device. This could be useful in giving the greyhound a 'refresher run' after a long spell of chasing in races where he catches nothing. Even more so, the lure could be very helpful in training young puppies for racing especially the difficult ones, which so often get unsighted when first introduced to dummy hares. The turning and twisting of the Lure Tronic would give the puppy more incentive to chase.

There are Lure Tronic systems in Canada and South Africa as well as in the USA. The American Sighthound Field Association, was formed in May 1972.

Cramp: A muscular complaint, quite frequently seen on the racing track – and in coursing greyhounds. It can be due to one of several known conditions such as inadequate training before strenuous exercise like coursing or racing and your vet should be consulted. One of the most common causes, in the racing greyhound, is over-dosing with cod liver oil. This is very rich in vitamin A and, if you give too much or for too long a period, it can cause trouble with a dog's muscles or bones, simply by killing off the other vitamins which he needs. In this case, the dog should be taken off the cod liver oil and given a course of vitamin E. Your vet may suggest that he has a course of injections of this vitamin, which will be quicker than the capsules in putting the matter right. It is essential that the dog be cured if he is to race, for he may run well in a trial and then have cramp during a race, which would, naturally, make most racing managers reluctant to grade him in races.

Cruft's: Acknowledged as the finest and most important dog show in the world which has gone from strength to strength since it was founded by Charles Cruft in 1886.

People come from all over the world to see the exhibits, which are scrutinized by the foremost judges of the show world before the coveted prizes are awarded. Vast numbers of viewers are also able to see parts of this show through the medium of television.

In 1891, when extra space was needed for Cruft's show, it was held at the Royal Agricultural Hall, Islington, in London, where it was held each year until 1938. In 1938, at the age of eighty-six, Charles Cruft died and the show was then taken over by the Kennel Club, in London. Since then, with the exception of the Second World War years, it has been held each year at Olympia.

From 1975 the show has been organized by Cruft's Committee. The Chairman is Sir Dudley Forwood, director of the Royal Show, and the committee comprises nine gentlemen and eight ladies, all selected by people associated with various canine groups and societies, plus eighteen nominees of the Kennel Club Committee.

1980 Season: Judge for greyhounds was Mrs Catherine Sutton. In a class of nine entries, including six champions, Parson's Ch. Rebuky's Poth was judged Best of Breed Dog; Wilton-Clark's Ch. Shalfleet Sarah Fraser was judged Best of Breed Bitch.

1980 winners were as follows:

Class Junior Dog
1st Jones' — Torveld Azurite
2nd Snook's — Torveld Linarite

Class Post Graduate Dog
1st Minn's & Willey's — Exhurst Englebert
2nd Bartlett's — Exhurst Snow White Brown
3rd Henry's — Windspiel Northern Legend

Class Limit Dog
1st Minn's & Willey's — Solstrand Pall Mall of Exhurst
2nd Davidson's — Wenonah the Virginian
3rd Newsham's — Shalfleet Silent Monarch

Class Open Dog
1st & C. C. Parson's — Ch. Rebuky's Poth (Best of Breed)
2nd & Reserve C. C. Mrs Dagmar Kenis's — Ch. Solstrand Double Diamond
3rd Wilton-Clark's — Ch. Shalfleet Spartacist

Class Junior Bitch
1st Lowe's — Shaun Valley Mystique
2nd Meakin's — Playama First Ghia

Class Post Graduate Bitch
1st Bartlett's — Exhurst Charming Style
2nd Fowles-Smith's — Harestreak Impudence
3rd Hibbs' — Wenonah June Folly

Class Limit Bitch
1st Minn's & Willey's — Exhurst Enchantress
2nd Snook's — Ro Perfyth
3rd Boissevain's — Branwen Hesper

Class Open Bitch
1st & C. C. Wilton-Clark's — Ch. Shalfleet Sarah Fraser
2nd Parson's — Reaching Pentewan
3rd Minn's — Ch. Roweth Powes of Exhurst

Cryptorchidism: When neither of a dog's testicles descends into the scrotum. A defect unacceptable in the show ring. Although the dog is unable to reproduce, the fault may pass on to progeny of any of his litter brother and sisters.

Cytacon (Vitamin B12): A tonic widely prescribed for human beings, as well as dogs, is taken orally. If the dog is run-down and out of condition Cytamen may be given, by injection. This acts much faster – going straight into the blood stream. Both products, from the Glaxo Laboratories, can be obtained from any chemist or druggist, without prescription. The dose of Cytacon for an adult greyhound is 1 dessertspoonful twice daily. Cytamen is supplied in small glass ampoules, of up to 1,000 c.c.s in each. Your vet will advise you on the use of this.

Daily Mirror Grand National, 1980: The final was run at the White City Stadium over the 500 metres course. Winner of the £4,000 prize was Gilt Edge Flyer (Bk dog 1976). Sire: Monalee Expert; Dam: Proud Secretary. Time of race: 30.22 secs. Owners: Arthur and Marjorie Wichello. Trainer: E. Pateman (Pte).

Damage: The owner of a dog which causes an accident or does serious damage is responsible for the cost of such damage. It is wise to take out a third party insurance to cover such an eventuality.

Deafness: Not a complaint greyhounds normally suffer from except, perhaps, when they are very old. Acute hearing is especially essential to the racing greyhound for he gets used to the sound of the mechanical 'hare' in transit, and can judge when it is approaching the traps which enables him to make a fast 'break'; always an asset in racing.

Dew Claws: Breeders usually have the dew claws removed from the show-bred greyhounds within a day or two of their birth. This is best done by a veterinary surgeon. There are two schools of thought as to whether the dew claws should be removed from racing and coursing dogs. Some veterinary surgeons say they are unsightly, useless and a source of bother when injured, but others say they afford a great deal of protection to the greyhound when turning at speed. I agree with the latter. I think dew claws often take a great deal of the strain which, otherwise, would go directly to the wrist.

Diarrhoea: Frequent watery motions, varying in colour from white to black to green. As soon as the trouble is noticed, give one dessertspoonful of castor oil. This does good and usually effects a cure. Give three activated charcoal tablets and then give two about every eight hours.

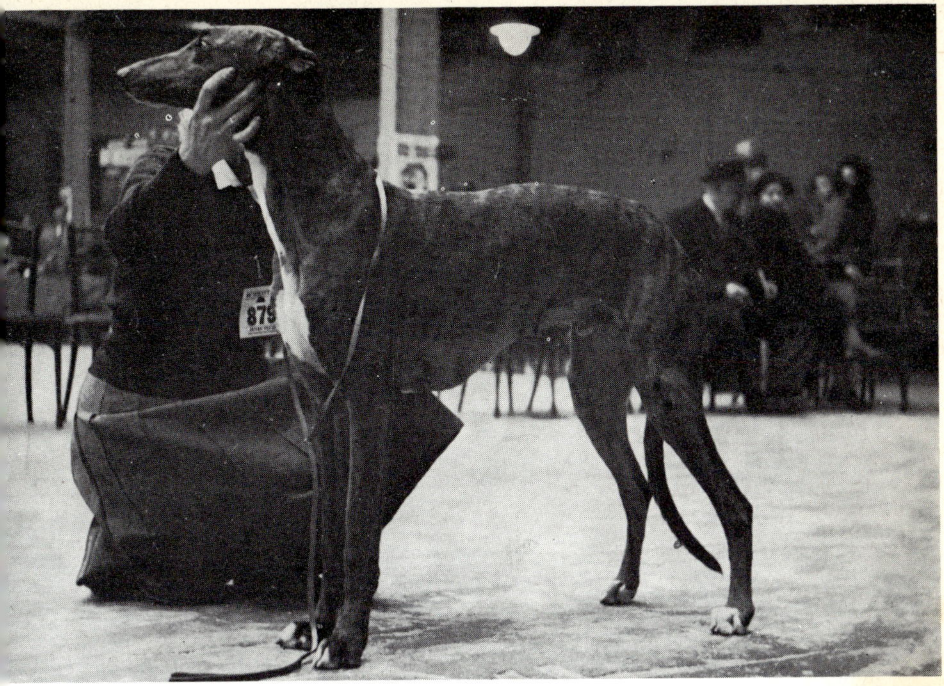

. (*above*): Ch. Treetops
lawk in the ring with Mrs
lella Smith. Owned by Mrs
udy de Casembroot (*By per-
iission of the owner*)

. Mrs Judy de Casembroot
ith her Ch. Treetops Golden
alcon, son of Ch. Treetops
lawk (*By permission of the
wner*)

7. Shadowland's Delight, whelped in June 1945 and owned by the author. Winner of the 1946 Trafalgar Cup

8. Shadowland's Delight winning a heat of the 1947 Wembley Summer Cup (*By permission of Racecourse Technical Services Ltd*)

Diet should be light – beaten egg whites may be given, milk made into a gruel with arrowroot and Benger's Food in equal parts and allowed to cool. After two days, if the trouble has cleared up, raw beef cut very fine may be given with some well-boiled rice, and the rice water may be given. If it is just a mild upset the trouble should have cleared up, but if the diarrhoea persists, take the dog's temperature and consult your vet. If there is a germ in the bowel, your vet should be able to prescribe one of the new and very effective tablets available.

Disinfectants: The air in kennels should never be heavy with the strong smell of disinfectants. Always use a good brand, well diluted, such as Dettol or a similar mild disinfectant. It is best to keep racing kennels clean and fresh with TCP, and this added to water is also a protection for the animals feet.

Dislocations: The displacement of a joint which can usually be felt to be out of place. Your vet should be consulted as it is often advisable to have an X-ray before there is much manipulation.

Most common in racing and coursing greyhounds is dislocation of the toe joints. The joint is painful and swollen; the dog is lame and often cannot put his foot to the ground. In the case of recent dislocation, the reduction is not difficult; the toe should be pulled straight with the fingers of one hand and with the other hand, the bone can be pressed into place.

Even if the dog is kept from all strenuous exercise, the displacement is likely to recur unfortunately. In a mild case, the cutting-back of the toe nail will be sufficient to help the healing of the joint. If more serious, it may be necessary to remove the first joint of the toe. Either operation should be carried out by your veterinary surgeon.

Distemper and Hard Pad: These are virus diseases which can be avoided completely by inoculations at an early time in a puppy's life. The 1940s and early 1950s must have been the greyhound breeders' most costly time, as hundreds of promising puppies and young dogs died. If they did recover most of them were left with disastrous, and usually incurable, after-effects. Thanks to improved research and its results, these diseases are now almost unknown, when compared with the dreadful scourge they were in former years.

Distemper and hard pad seem to go together. The pads become very hard and cracked; this is probably due to the very high temperature which goes with the disease. Dogs perspire through their pads (*see* PORES).

If a dog seems dull and listless, always take his temperature. The first symptom of distemper is a rise in temperature and, if this is two or three degrees above normal (101.5°F.) then something is wrong and the vet should be called. If the temperature persists then it must be reduced and the best thing for this is aspirin. Give two aspirin tablets and, if the temperature has not gone down, give two more tablets half an hour later. The bowels should be kept open and, if necessary give one mild dose of castor oil and syrup of buckthorn (1 tablespoonful in equal parts).

An emetic (a piece of common soda about the size of a hazel-nut for a puppy and almost twice as large for an adult dog) put on the back of the tongue and pushed gently down may help to get rid of much of the mucous and catarrh which, in this dreadful disease, seems to invade the whole body. The dog should be isolated and, if it is distemper, other symptoms will soon follow such as loss of appetite and condition, a husky cough and perhaps vomiting. The eyes become very weak and should be gently bathed with an eye lotion. There is not always diarrhoea, but always a discharge from the nose, although this may not appear until later. Although the temperature may temporarily fall to normal within two or three days, the fever will quickly return. The patient should be kept warm and free from draughts, but not in an airless stuffy atmosphere, which will do him more harm than good. If the weather is not warm, he needs clothing. (*See* NURSING.)

In all illnesses, but especially this one, nursing plays a very great part in the outcome. Unless someone has nursed a dog through this killer disease, it is almost impossible to imagine the misery it causes. Any, or all, of the lungs, brain and the nervous system are attacked. The whole of the inside of the dog appears to be over-run by catarrh or mucous, which oozes from the eyes and the nose and can be heard bubbling all over the body.

It won't be easy to tempt him to eat. Frequently offer him food and, if necessary, leave it with him for a little while. A lap or two will even help. Dogs are inclined to get thirsty with distemper so offer him bread and milk or chicken or rabbit broth with a little of the meat. Also suitable are cooked fish with a little of the juice, Brand's Essence (beef or chicken flavour), milky gruel made with Benger's Food, Slippery Elm or Robinson's groats. Some vets advise against giving water, but boiled and cooled water is all right.

The dog should not be allowed out of his kennel until he has fully recovered, and his temperature has been normal for three days or so. If the lungs are affected, someone the dog knows should go into the kennel or room, with a bowl of steaming hot water to which some

Friar's Balsam and menthol (made up by the chemist) has been added. With a blanket over both dog's and owner's heads, the dog will find great relief by inhaling the steam – and it won't do his helper any harm!

Dogs which have pneumonia, as a symptom of this disease, have a good chance of getting over it without any disastrous side-effects. It doesn't often seem to go with the worst complication of all, which is when the nervous system is attacked (the brain or spinal cords and their membranes). The final outcome is almost always Chorea (St Vitus's Dance) with fits, blindness and whole or partial paralysis. These effects sometimes subside when the dog becomes stronger, but are almost always incurable.

Dosing: (*see* Fig. 4-5) If giving medicine in liquid form, do not open the dog's mouth and pour on to the tongue. Raise the head slightly, pull one side of the cheek out gently to make a pouch, and pour a small quantity at a time into the pouch. If he doesn't want to swallow, gently pinch his nose, and he will try to breathe through his mouth and the medicine will go down.

To give a pill, slightly raise the dog's head, open his mouth and put it on the back of his tongue, gently pushing the pill down into the throat. Close the dog's mouth and he will swallow the pill.

Drugs (wrongful use of): It is argued by some people that a drug administered by a vet for a specific reason and detected by chromatography testing, should not necessarily mean the withdrawal of a greyhound from his race. Whether a drug be given as a necessary cure for some affliction, or for criminal purposes, it will still have the same effect on a dog if he is raced; to make him run faster or slower than he normally can. Apart from depriving the public of 'fair wagering', there can be disastrous results to the dog and/or his companions, through his abnormal running during the race. If a test proves 'positive' a dog should be withdrawn from his race whatever the reason for the presence of the drug.

Duchy of Cornwall, Feudal Dues: On 19 November 1973, Prince Charles received his feudal dues, as Duke of Cornwall, in the grounds of Launceston Castle. This castle, built by the Normans, dates from ancient times when Launceston was the capital of Cornwall.

On behalf of the Manor of Elerky, Veryan, a brace of beautiful greyhounds was accepted by Prince Charles. The greyhounds, Whisky and Soda, were loaned for the occasion by Mr and Mrs R. H. Parsons, of Egloshayle, Wadebridge, and were returned to them (as is usual these days) after the ceremony.

An old charter, under which certain lands are held in the Duchy of

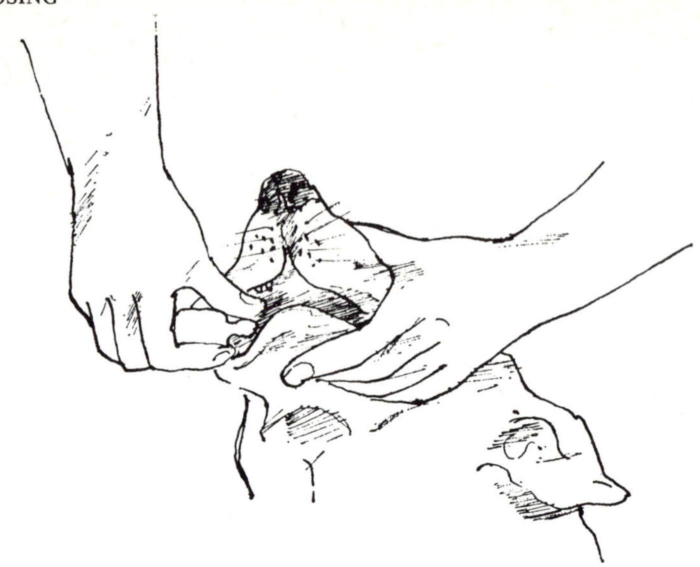

Fig. 4 How to administer medicine or liquid to a greyhound

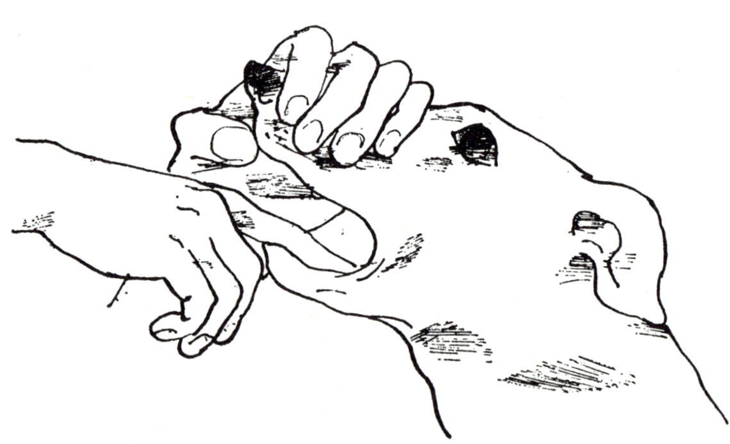

Fig. 5 How to give a pill to a greyhound

Cornwall, decrees that these feudal dues be delivered to the Duke of Cornwall, as part of the terms of tenure. The previous dues were accepted by Prince Charles's grandfather, King George VI, as Duke of Cornwall.

Ear Care: Because these lie close to the head, greyhounds seldom have trouble with their ears. Although I have had charge of hundreds of greyhounds, I have never put any loose powder or oil in their ears and, when I have seen this done, it has always appeared to do more harm than good. At times, the ears do need to be cleansed, as they become dirty and dusty inside, but it is best to soak a piece of clean cotton gauze in some warm water, to which has been added a little Peroxide of Hydrogen. Wring this out and with about two thicknesses on an orange stick, or the little finger, wipe very gently the inside crevices of the ear. Dry gently with a clean piece of dry gauze. Do not use cotton wool for ears. If the ears are very dirty, the same thing may be done with almond oil (as it is the only oil which will not clog) but it is essential that the oil be wrung out from the gauze so that it does not run into the ears.

Greyhounds' ears should be soft and silky but sometimes, through surfeit or eczema, the edges are thick with what is dried serum being exuded. This needs treating internally but it will help to mix a little almond oil with some oxide of zinc ointment and gently rub on the edges of the ears.

Eclampsia: (*see* PARTURIENT ECLAMPSIA).

Eczema: There are many forms of this, and almost all non-contagious skin troubles come under this heading. Often they are more difficult to cure because there is no parasite to be defined and acted upon. Eczema is often a disease of malnutrition, mainly through worms taking the nourishment from the food which is meant to keep the dog in health. Surfeit (or over-heating) is another cause. The latter is usually due to improper feed, and both eczema and surfeit mainly need treatment from the inside. Symptoms are similar to those in the case of mange: irritable skin, the dog frequently scratching, licking and biting himself. The cure is prolonged when dirt gets in the sore places when the skin becomes broken. Often a bleeding tail, a discharging eye, or nose, will get rid of the serum and may prevent this from 'breaking out' through the skin. When the serum is discharging through the ear only, the trouble takes longer to clear up, but this serum will always force its way out through the thinnest parts of the skin and will sometimes come through the eruption of the toes. Bathe with warm water, without any disinfectant, and wipe away any serum.

Treatment should be as follows: first make sure the dog has no worms. Give a 1 oz dose of Epsom or Glauber Salts twice a week. Melt these in a little hot water and add a spoonful of honey and, when cool, the dog will usually lap it up. Change the diet immediately you notice any signs of eczema or surfeit. Give him food which is easily assimilated (digested). Avoid salt and starchy foods, making his food principally of raw meat. After two doses of the Epsom or Glauber Salts give no more laxatives, but include raw or underdone liver in his diet. Over-heating foods and gravies should not be given for a time. Remember, if the dog is scratching, he will need extra food, as irritation will take a great deal out of him.

Enema: Enemas are of various kinds and used for various purposes, purgative, nutritive, sedative, stimulative, as a vermifuge, or for convulsions.

In cases of stoppage of the bowels, purgative or laxative enemas are necessary; they are also very useful to relieve constipation. For dogs that are very ill, it is much better to give a small enema rather than a dose of purgative medicine as the latter often causes sickness, which should be avoided when the patient is weak. To cause an action of the bowels in cases of constipation only a small enema is required – 2 teaspoonfuls of glycerine mixed with about 8 tablespoonfuls of warm water. Instead of glycerine, soapy water may be used or olive oil blood-heat of 100° or 101°F.

In cases of real obstruction of the bowels, give double the quantities as those of simple constipation and, in these cases, the enema should be given three times a day. For greyhounds one of the larger enema syringes is best. The bone point of the syringe should be well smeared with Vaseline, and then the whole length of this (about two inches) can be passed into the rectum. *Care* should be taken when using an enema not to pump a lot of air into the bowel, so it is essential that the syringe is filled with the fluid before passing the bone end into the rectum. (*See* SUPPOSITORIES.)

Nutritive Enemas: Peptonized milk, beef tea and eggs beaten up and about 4 oz given to the patient every four hours.

English Greyhound Derby: Winners of the English Greyhound Derby run at White City Stadium, Wood Lane, London:

Year	*Winner*	*Year*	*Winner*
1927	ENTRY BADGE	1931	SELDOM LED
1928	BOHER ASH	1932	WILD WOOLLEY
1929	MICK THE MILLER	1933	FUTURE CUTLET
1930	MICK THE MILLER	1934	DAVESLAND

Year	*Winner*	*Year*	*Winner*
1935	GRETA RANEE (bitch)	1958	PIGALLE WONDER
1936	FINE JUBILEE	1959	MILE BUSH PRIDE
1937	WATTLE BARK	1960	DULEEK DANDY
1938	LONE KEEL	1961	PALMS PRINTER
1939	HIGHLAND RUM	1962	THE GRAND CANAL
1940*	G. R. ARCHDUKE	1963	LUCKY BOY BOY
1941	No race due to war	1964	HACK UP CHIEFTAIN
1942	No race due to war	1965	CHITTERING CLAPTON
1943	No race due to war	1966	FAITHFUL HOPE
1944	No race due to war	1967	TRIC TRAC
1945	BALLYHENNESSY SEAL	1968	CAMIRA FLASH
1946	MONDAYS NEWS	1969	SAND STAR
1947	TREV'S PERFECTION	1970	JOHN SILVER
1948	PRICELESS BORDER	1971	DOLORES ROCKET (bitch)
1949	NARROGAR ANN (bitch)	1972	PATRICIA'S HOPE
1950	BALLYMAC BALL	1973	PATRICIA'S HOPE
1951	BALLYLANIGAN TANIST	1974	JIMSUN
1952	ENDLESS GOSSIP†	1975	TARTAN KHAN
1953	DAW'S DANCER	1976	MUTTS SILVER
1954	PAUL'S FUN	1977	BALLINSKA BAND
1955	RUSHTON MAC	1978	LACCA CHAMPION
1956	DUNMORE KING	1979	SARAH'S BUNNY
1957	FORD SPARTAN		

*(race held at Harringay Stadium)
†(son of the 1948 and 1949 Derby winners)

England's 1974 Derby winner, Jimsun, received £13,500 – then the richest prize money in the greyhound racing world – when the entry fee for each contestant was £100.

England's 1980 Jubilee Derby (fifty years since its inception) was again sponsored by Spillers. The entry fee was £200 and the 500 metres final, as usual, took place at London's White City Stadium, on 28th June. Still the richest prize money in the greyhound racing world, the six finalists shared a purse of £50,000. £35,000 went to the winner, £7,500 to the second, £3,000 to the third and £1,500 each to the remaining three.

The winner was Indian Joe (Bk dog – Sept. 1977). Sire: Brave Bran; Dam: Minnatonka. Owned by Mr Alfie McLean. Trained by John Hayes (Ireland). Time: 29.68 secs.

Second was Hurry On Bran (Bd dog – May 1978). Sire: Brave Bran; Dam: Hurry On Hostess. Owned by Mr Eddie Costello. Trained by Eric Pateman (Wimbledon).

Third was Young Breeze (Fawn bitch – May 1978). Sire: Sage; Dam: Scorduff Breeze. Owned and trained by Jack Coker (Oxford).

Indian Joe was the fifth Irish-trained greyhound to win the Derby. He is the fourth successive seeded wide-runner to win this Classic and the sixth, in this category, in the last ten years. As the only seeded wide-runner in the 1980 final, Indian Joe was automatically allotted trap six.

Breaking clear on the outside of the field, he had a trouble-free run leaving the other five runners, trap-positioned by draw, to overcome the hazards of racing. (*See* SEEDING OF WIDE RUNNERS IN OPEN RACES.)

Enteritis (Inflammation of the bowels): This usually affects both the small and large intestines and is either acute catarrhal or chronic catarrhal.

Acute: Caused by improper, or too much, food; organic or mineral poisons; sudden changes in the weather and certain nervous conditions – also from some diseases such as distemper, dysentery and septicaemia.

Symptoms: Diarrhoea, thin watery motions; sometimes sickness, a quickened pulse and slight rise in temperature, with abdominal pain. These symptoms usually lessen after treatment for diarrhoea and the dog recovers within a few days.

Chronic: This form is far more serious than the acute and the chances of recovery are slim. If the dog does recover the cure takes weeks instead of days. Chronic enteritis may follow the acute form and is more likely to be seen in very bad cases of disease such as distemper. The mucous discharge from the bowel increases and shreds of the membrane may be passed, which is a very bad sign. The pulse is quiet and, as the disease advances, becomes weak and 'thready'. The motions are frequent, sometimes diarrhoea and sometimes constipation. Pain on pressure of the abdomen and the intestines may be easily felt because the bowels are inflamed and swollen. The patient becomes anaemic and wasted, the breath is foul and the tongue rusty-red in colour. Ulcers may form in the mouth.

The diet should consist principally of milk – plain or with Bengers Food to which a little meat juice may be added. Plain, unboiled, milk may be given with the white of an egg. Later scraped raw meat may be given. The diet should be given little and often. Treatment will be given by your vet.

European Greyhound Racing Championship: This race is run in a different country each year. It has so far been contested by greyhounds from Austria, Belgium, Czechoslovakia, Denmark, Finland, France, West Germany, Holland, Norway, Sweden and Switzerland.

Impallah, a bitch from Holland, won the event three years in succession: 1962 (Austria); 1963 (Switzerland) and 1964 (Holland). In Western Europe greyhound racing is run under club rules – without prize money.

Exercise, for Puppies Destined for the Track or Coursing: Apart from freedom in a large paddock with an ever-open kennel door, puppies should, from an early age, be allowed freedom to gallop at their own pace sometime during the day. They will follow over a field or open ground and will not need to be taken on leads and collars.

Six months of age is early enough to get them used to these, unless it is necessary to take them any distance for their exercise before you can let them loose. For the first few weeks of training to lead and collar, they may have to have a smaller narrow collar and shorter lead, until their necks are thick enough for them to wear the fish-tail collar and long lead (*see* COLLARS AND LEADS). The infallible way to 'break' to the lead and collar is, first, to put a collar on the puppy whilst in the paddock and leave it on, say, for half a day. Then leave the puppy, or the litter, with collars on for a whole day. It then, quite cheerfully, allows the lead to be attached to the collar, and go off for a walk, which seems to prove that it is the collar it isn't too fond of at first. Walking with their mother to lead is quite a good idea, or with an older good-tempered greyhound, but never start off with too many, and never lose patience when it is most required – when the puppy is learning.

Puppies will take plenty of exercise in the paddock, if given an old sack or rug to pull around and shake. As greyhounds today, more than ever, are wanted to 'stay' in their races, it is essential that they have enough freedom to develop their lungs and muscles. What isn't achieved before birth and during the first six months of their lives, can never be accomplished later. It is essential that they get used to noise and bustle and for the first taste of this, once they are able to wear the safe fish-tail collars and leather leads, it is a good idea to take them to a dual carriage-way. Find one where there is a grass verge and, further in, a pathway where they may walk. They then see and hear the traffic without it appearing to be coming straight at them. At nine months of age the youngsters should be taken from the paddock and paired in kennels because, at this age, they are not so likely to take the necessary exercise in paddocks, but will come fresh from their kennels to walk or gallop. If the owners have no ground on which to gallop the dogs, it is possible to take them *very early* to parks or open spaces for their exercise, once the dogs are properly lead-trained.

The road walks should now be increased to one in the morning and one in the afternoon, and grooming should begin. Whilst loose in the paddock, puppies should not be groomed as they need all the natural oil in their coats to resist weather conditions. When the puppies are living in the kennels, it is essential that after the last meal or drink they should be allowed in the paddock if only for a few minutes.

The puppies should be shown a skin to shake and get interested in. First, they may be shown this by tying to a thin cord a rabbit skin, or anything fluffy, with the other end of the cord tied to the top of a thin pole. Hold the pole, with the other end on the ground, and swing so that the rabbit skin rotates in a wide circle. The puppy should automatically chase this and try to get hold of it.

Eye Dropper: Obtainable from chemists and druggists. Useful for the eyes and in the use of some medicines or for feeding baby puppies.

False Heat: Does sometimes occur and can be very misleading as the bitch may even allow mating. The discharge appears normal, as in a true 'heat', but when it is false the true period generally makes its appearance from a week to a month afterwards. The bitch can then be mated if a litter is required.

False Pregnancy: If this does occur, it is usually in highly hysterical and nervous bitches. They behave in every respect as though they are in whelp and often look as though they will have quite a large litter but, by the time the puppies are due, nothing but a little discharge appears and the bitch gradually goes back to her normal shape. The milk may have to be removed or the mammary glands rubbed twice a day with either equal parts of methylated spirit and water, or gin and water. (*See* LACTATION, EXCESSIVE.)

Famous Greyhounds:

DOLORES ROCKET ('Cindy')

'Cindy' is the daughter of the great sire, Newdown Heather; her dam Come on Dolores was also the daughter of a great sire, Knockhill Chieftain. She is owned by the White Brothers.

'Cindy' was voted top English Greyhound bitch of 1970 and top English greyhound of 1971, winning the English Derby, the St Leger, the Essex Vase, the Wimbledon Spring Cup, the Cindy Trophy, Wembley Spring Cup, the Puppy Oaks, the Crayford Spring Cup and the Puppy

Championship. In only ten months of racing, 'Cindy' won £16,000 plus trophies valued at £1,000, a record for prize money as well as racing achievements.

Best winning times were: the Puppy Oaks, 500 yards, Wimbledon 27.85 secs; the Cairns Memorial, 500 yards, Wimbledon 27.71 secs; the Wimbledon Spring Cup, 700 yards, 39.65 secs; the St Leger, 700 yards, Wembley 30.29 secs; the English Derby, 525 yards, White City 28.61 secs; the Wembley Spring Cup, 525 yards, 29.09 secs; the Essex Vase, 650 yards, Romford 36.06 secs; the Cindy Trophy, 700 yards, Wimbledon 39.58 secs; and the Spring Cup, 700 yards, Crayford, 40.72 secs.

Wherever 'Cindy' raced, the crowds came to see her. Her fan-mail was considerable, coming from all parts of the world – Australia, Ireland, Sweden, the United Kingdom and the USA. After running in the Cesarewitch at West Ham, when she pulled a muscle, she was rested for some time but, owing to this injury, she had to be retired.

NEWDOWN HEATHER

Owned by Mr George Posnett and Mrs Kathleen McKee. Weight 90 lb.

This great-hearted dog, who was whelped in 1964, won many top racing and coursing events in Ireland. After winning the Jack Wick Cup and the Puppy Cup at Dunmore, it was obvious that he was an outstanding performer and a large sum of money was offered for him – but refused.

His appearance in the English Derby was eagerly awaited but, although he ran in trials, he was kept out of the classic because of a fractured toe. In Ireland he again went on to add to his many successes in both racing and coursing events. Finally winning the Ulster Cup, at the Coursing Club's meeting, he was then retired to stud owing to the recurrence of an old injury.

What was a great loss to racing and coursing, proved the gain of all time to the breeding world. It is impossible to give here a list of all the events won by his progeny – it would be easier to give a list of the races they haven't won! Winter Hope and Moordyke Spot were two of his outstanding sons in England. When Moordyke Spot was voted top dog of 1970, Newdown Heather's young daughter Dolores Rocket was voted bitch of the year. Crefogue Flash, winner of the Puppy Derby at Wimbledon, was another outstanding son of his. He won the *Sporting Life* Puppy Championship at Wimbledon, with Dolores Rocket a close second and third was Super Fun. All three were sired by Newdown Heather.

SHERRY'S PRINCE ('Nooky')

Owned by Mrs Joyce Matthews. Weight 75 lb.

Trainer John Shevlin discovered the wonder hurdler, Sherry's Prince, but he died without seeing the final proof of this dog's amazing ability to become the hurdler of the century. It was Colin West (now trainer at the White City, London) who trained and took 'Nooky' through his journey to the top and John Shevlin would have been the first to admit that he himself could have done no better.

After winning his first hurdles race in May 1969, 'Nooky' went on to amass a total of thirty wins by April 1970 – five of which were record-breaking runs. These included the English Grand National, run at the White City, London, and a heat of the Scottish Grand National. It was in the final of this latter race when he met with disaster and although coming second, broke his hock.

Very few dogs win races of consequence after breaking a hock but, thanks to the skill of the White City Veterinary Surgeon, 'Nooky' came back in October to carry on from where he left off. From then until July 1971 he won another twenty-two races, including another English Grand National and the Wimbledon Gold Cup, shattering five more track records. Once again, misfortune overtook him during a race at the White City, when he left part of his tail behind in the first-bend wire. In September he returned to racing to show what he could do despite a depleted tail. He went on to break another six track records whilst winning a further nineteen races. These included his third English Grand National and the Midland Grand National. When he retired in April 1972 he had won seventy-one races, of which he had broken the existing track records in sixteen.

WESTPARK MUSTARD

Sire: Newdown Heather; Dam: April Merry. July 1971 W & Bk bitch.

Owned by Mr Cyril Scotland and trained by Tom Johnston at Wembley Stadium, she shattered Mick the Miller's forty-four year old English record when she won the 'Mick the Miller Record Stakes' at Wembley Stadium on Monday evening 28 October 1974. This was her twentieth consecutive win – beating Mick's nineteen runs. (The world record is held by America's Huntsman who notched a total of twenty-seven straight runs.)

On 6 November 1974 it was hoped that Westpark Mustard would notch her twenty-first consecutive win, when she visited Ireland's Shelbourne Park (Dublin) to compete in the Carroll's Challenge Stakes, but she was beaten into second place. Ireland's champion, Tommy Astaire (especially noted for his terrific early pace) was well in the lead at the first bend, and held this position throughout the race. At one point Westpark Mustard was baulked when she tried to make her run but, even so, it seemed to be generally accepted that she would not have beaten the winner over this distance.

Carroll's Challenge Stakes – 600 yards flat Shelbourne Park, Dublin.

1st	Tommy Astaire	price 3/1	Trap 1
2nd	Westpark Mustard	Evens fav.	6
3rd	Dal's Birthday	12/1	4
4th	Ballinatin Boy	5/2	3

Time: 33.31 secs. Distances: 5½ l. ½ l. 1½ l.
Prize Money: £1,500. Tommy Astaire trained by Paddy Keane, Ireland.

Feeding: White bread should not be fed to dogs as it can cause hysteria and scouring. Stale wholemeal or Hovis bread is the best – but should not be given sooner than five days from baking. There are also good biscuits and biscuit meal on the market, and one of the best of these is Winalot. I am told that much of the bread sold today and marked 'brown' is only white bread with colouring matter added – so be sure it is wholemeal you are buying. Rusk is made by slicing the bread and drying it out in an oven at low heat, until it is a golden brown and snaps when broken. This is especially good for both puppies and grown dogs since it keeps their teeth in order without having to give them bones.

Dogs require concentrated food and from six months of age half their diet should be of meat. At six months they require two main meals a day. Breakfast, smaller than the afternoon meal, should consist of one raw fresh egg with one teaspoonful of Virol or honey for each puppy; the eggs may be given unbeaten and the dogs may have more than one each; add to warm milk and feed. Then give them puppy biscuits, or dry rusk, to crunch. Olive oil is good for the coat and may be given once or twice a week in place of the honey or Virol. In this case, one teaspoonful of oil should be added to each egg and should be beaten until the oil disappears into the eggs; then add to the warm milk. Raw eggs – but they must be fresh – are great promoters of growth and are very good for greyhounds. Free-range eggs are better than battery eggs.

The late afternoon feed is best prepared by first soaking the biscuit meal, or stale bread, in cold water and then squeezing the meal out as dry as possible by hand. To this, add the warm gravy to make it moist but not sloppy. Three times a week add raw meat (allowing one pound for each puppy) also a teaspoonful of Bemax. On other afternoons, substitute fish boiled or steamed, using the juice to moisten the bread. If you live near the sea, it is possible to get cod heads, or conger eel heads, which boil into a jelly and, when the bones are removed, it can be added to the bread and makes a most nourishing meal. Other alternatives are meat from cooked sheep or ox heads, cooked hearts, tripe or sheep paunches – all of which are very nourishing. Pork should never be fed to dogs.

Dogs' stomachs are not conducive towards digesting boiled vegetables and these are best left alone. A little raw scraped carrot or finely chopped raw cabbage stump, watercress or a segment of garlic chopped can be added to the food, and all these are good for them. Potatoes, in one respect, are very good. After an illness, a meal of very well cooked potatoes – mashed as one would make for oneself – will cleanse and remove all catarrh and mucous from the stomach. Liver is good for dogs but should not be fed too often as it relaxes the bowels – once a week is a good idea – and a little raw liver may be given as a laxative.

The amount of food required is said to be governed by a dog's breathing capacity. A very useful assessment of the food required by a greyhound used to be half an ounce of food for every pound weight of the dog, and that the last three ribs (tail end) should always be seen. Whilst this still seems to be the case with the top open-race greyhounds, very many of the others seem to be built for comfort rather than speed – it is often necessary to dig deep to find out whether they still possess ribs!

Dogs' gastric juices are very much stronger than those of human beings and, except when they are very young, it is not necessary to mince meat to feed them. They can easily digest quite large pieces of meat and, in fact, are better for doing so.

In its natural state a dog would kill its quarry and eat practically the whole of the kill, including offal and roughage, thus getting all the vitamins necessary. Having been domesticated for so long, it is necessary to try and give a balanced diet through the artificial feeding.

Proteins are tissue-forming and supply the energy required. In a working greyhound this is a very important factor and possibly why, with top racing dogs, often the only flesh given is fed raw.

Carbohydrates give warmth to the body and the power necessary for muscular action. Animals, like humans, require an ample supply of vitamins, but these are best coming from the food rather than fed separately. An overdose of one vitamin in the body can destroy the

9. Ireland's Newdown Heather, the greatest sire of this decade. His progeny are world famous as winners of many classic and open races and coursing events (*By permission of the owners, Mr George Posnett and Mrs Kathleen McKee*)

10. Mrs Dagmas Kenis's show greyhound, Ch. Solstrand Double Diamond, winner of 14 C.C.s (*By permission of the owner*)

11. HRH Prince Philip, president of the NPFA, is seen accepting Playfield Royal from Mr Ken Tucker (right). On the left of the picture is Brighton trainer Gordon Hodson, who has charge of the dog. Playfield Royal's prize money is donated to the fund (*By permission of the Greyhound Racing Association*)

other necessary vitamins. A food such as Virol (rich in bone-marrow) is a great conditioner in correcting diet deficiency. There are many things which can be given, but unless these can be easily assimilated they may do more harm than good.

Feeding During Training and Pre-Racing: Feeding during training should be of that which gives the body strongly developed muscles, energy and everything required for the purpose. All the necessary ingredients are found in flesh and bread.

Bread should be wholemeal fed after five days from baking – unless rusked. Mutton is the best meat, beef the next best and horse flesh next – all to be fed lean. Horseflesh must be free from drugs and is the most likely meat to contain these since it is seldom used for human consumption, and the animal may have been treated for a suspected complaint before slaughter. Horseflesh is best fed raw, grilled or baked. The gravy from this should not be given as it is too oily. Beef may be fed raw or cooked. Fat should be skimmed from the cooked meat and the gravy used to soak rusk or bread.

Tasty biscuits may be made for puppies or grown dogs, in the same proportions which can be used for bread – three parts wholemeal flour and one part oatmeal. Jelly from cooked cow heels is nourishing and can be added to the feed.

The evening before the race day the feed should be slightly smaller than usual. On the race day some people give the dog a light meal about 10.30 am and then nothing until the dog gets home late at night after racing (except a drink after his race). The trouble is, however, greyhounds love their food and expect their usual meals on the race day, so it may be advisable to give a *very small* early breakfast and then, before they start on their journey, a *small* drink of warm milk or tea to which a whole *new-laid* raw egg and a spoonful of glucose has been added. Dogs, like people, vary in what suits them, and this can only be found out by experience. Some people will not say how they feed their charges.

Fighters: A dog, which deliberately interferes with others during a race or official trial, is subject to disciplinary action and may be disqualified. If, in a race, the dog is disqualified, he forfeits any prize money which he might have won in that race, but the order of finish stands as regards betting. On disqualification the greyhound is not allowed to run in a race again unless he has been judged 'clean' in a series of trials with not less than four dogs. Should he interfere again and be disqualified, he is warned off all tracks under NGRC rules and he will have his name and particulars in the NGRC Calendar, where he will be declared a confirmed fighter.

Flapping Tracks: The name by which independent tracks always seem to have been known. (*See* INDEPENDENT TRACKS.)

Food Values: Approximate relative amounts of protein and carbohydrates contained in some foods are given below. Carbohydrates give temperature to the body and energy for muscular action. Protein forms tissue and gives force to the body.

Barley meal	10 parts protein	57 parts carbohydrates
Beef (lean)	10 parts protein	17 parts carbohydrates
Cow's milk	10 parts protein	30 parts carbohydrates
Hare and Rabbit	10 parts protein	5 parts carbohydrates
Horseflesh (lean)	10 parts protein	15 parts carbohydrates
Mutton (lean)	10 parts protein	19 parts carbohydrates
Oatmeal	10 parts protein	50 parts carbohydrates
Wheatflour	10 parts protein	46 parts carbohydrates

Form: The last three races or trials must appear on racecards. Some tracks provide more. Information is also given as to the type of runner, etc., whether a fast or slow starter, whether able to finish well, or whether it fades towards the finish of a race, and other factors as regards the state of going, times, etc. A dog running in an early race may be capable of a much faster time than if it runs in a later race, should it be known as a 'kennel-fretter'.

Fractures and Breaks: A broken limb will swing from the part where broken. There are three kinds of fractures. *Simple,* when one or more bones are broken in two pieces and without serious injury to the skin. *Compound,* when as well as fracture of the bones, the skin and other tissues are torn. *Comminutive,* when a bone is crushed into several pieces.

Most common among the racing and coursing greyhound is the broken hock and broken toes. It is essential to consult a vet at once if you suspect a fractured or broken bone. At all race meetings conducted under NGRC rules and coursing meetings under NCC rules, a qualified veterinary surgeon will be in attendance, and will give the treatment required by the patient until your own vet can take over. If no vet is present when the accident takes place some helpful first aid must be given by the one in charge of the dog. Keep the patient quiet in the best possible way and the break should be supported by an improvised splint. (*See* SPLINTS.) Two aspirins given to the dog will relieve any pain.

Free Service: (*see* STUD DOG).

Gangrene: This may follow improper treatment of a severe wound or from a too tightly bandaged leg in a case of fracture. It is most likely to occur in the greyhound when a tail bleeding at the tip is too tightly bound or secured and the circulation impaired. The parts are at first very swollen, red and painful, and later the skin turns black or blue. An offensive blood-coloured fluid oozes. The pain disappears later from the part, which becomes cold and clammy – turning green. In fact, the infected part dies. A vet should be consulted at once.

Germicides: These should never be used neat on the dog, but diluted with water. Where instructions are given to dilute the product, make it slightly weaker. Otherwise, a good germicide may become an irritant to the dog.

Gold Collar, The: Run at Catford Stadium, London SE6, the 1979 final of the greyhound classic was won by Gay Flash, over a distance of 555 metres in a time of 35.08 secs.

Gay Flash (Bd bitch – May 1977). Sire: Fionntra Frolic; Dam: London Child.

Owned by: Mr J. Goodwright. Trained by: Paddy Milligan (Catford Stadium).

Grading: The classification of runners by the racing manager, giving each a fair opportunity to win. Time is used as a basis for grading.

Going: The effect of weather changes on the track surface. A change in going usually means a variation of 'form' – depending on the greyhound's liking or disliking of the changes. Sprinters are usually favoured by a fast track and stayers are likely to benefit from a slow track. A wide-runner is favoured by muddy or heavy going, since it is the inside of the track which is in a bad state. When a track surface has to be covered by sand or peat, a front-runner may put up a better performance than would be supposed as he kicks up the loose surface into the faces of dogs that otherwise might have passed him.

Greyhound as a Companion: As a companion, the greyhound can have few rivals. Today, he is still the faithful, intelligent and devoted friend of man he has been for so many generations. Essentially a sporting dog, it is amazing, but true, that even after having known only a kennel life he will, when introduced to the house, immediately settle down as though he had always lived there, taking everything in his stride. Treat him as one of the family, find him an easy-chair, basket or bed (because not having a very dense coat, he will prefer to be off the ground), and once he has his special place to lie, he will go there and never be a nuisance.

As a walking companion he has no equal and will walk at your side for as many miles as you like. He is devoted to children and will spend many hours with them. When your greyhound has finished his career, whether coursing, racing or in the show ring, take care of him for the rest of his life and your only regret will be that this was far too short.

Many people have done much to help the unwanted greyhound and find him a home. Most of these unwanted greyhounds, regrettably, come from the racing world. It is the people who could well afford to see that their greyhounds are cared for until the end of their days who are often the worst offenders. Many good owners who have raced dogs and would still like to do so, often say they cannot afford to have racers now as they have the ex-racers to keep. Private trainers have always played their part in keeping some of the 'pensioners'.

For many years there have been suggestions, such as that the tracks should keep the greyhound when they are injured or too old to race and *they should if they own them*. The problem is the responsibility of *all* owners. There is now a great drive going on in the racing world to do something about this matter and money is being given from all quarters to ensure that these dogs do not go for vivisection or to so-called 'homes' where they spend a life of misery. This does not alter the fact that many owners still have strings of racers and leave people with far less money than they have to provide for their ex-racers, whilst they buy more dogs. Today, kennels and land cost vast amounts of money and, with all the other expenses of staff, food, etc., the costs snowball for an establishment housing even a small number of dogs, as most of them live to be at least thirteen years old.

If an extra fee of £10 were charged on every registration of a greyhound, both by the National Coursing Club and the National Greyhound Racing Club, this money could then go to a fund, with any other moneys collected, for the help of these retired racers without homes. Then, several people could be employed specially to travel and investigate the suitability of any home offered. Possibly the tracks would help by keeping a few of these dogs in their kennels whilst they are on the waiting list. Some of the contract trainers would be paid to do this if they have room in their kennels and would be willing to do so – all this would be far cheaper than setting up special kennels, which would never be adequate.

The people who really need investigating are those who apply for a dog, offering it a home. There are people who, after investigation, are refused their request for a dog. In the case of a child wanting a dog, make sure that the parents want it too, as it can be just a seven days' wonder to the child. The greyhound in his new life needs love, affection and care.

It is so often said, when finding a home for a greyhound, that it *must* go where there is plenty of space. This is not really true, for one may have hundreds of acres but this may not mean that the dog will be allowed to use them. So long as the dog is taken for a good walk each day, he will be happy. (*See* RETIRED GREYHOUND TRUST.)

Greyhound Derby: (*see* ENGLISH GREYHOUND DERBY, IRISH GREYHOUND DERBY, SPANISH GREYHOUND DERBY).

Greyhound Racecourses: Stadiums racing under NGRC rules are:

London Area: Catford; Hackney; Harringay; Walthamstow; Wembley; White City; Wimbledon.

Provinces: Birmingham (Hall Green); Birmingham (Perry Bar); Bletchley; Brighton; Bristol; Cambridge; Coventry; Cradley Heath; Crayford; Derby; Edinburgh; Glasgow; Gloucester; Gosforth; Hull; Leeds; Leicester; Manchester (Belle Vue); Manchester (White City); Middlesborough; Newcastle; Oxford; Poole (Dorset); Portsmouth; Ramsgate; Reading; Rochester; Romford; Sheffield; Slough; Southend; Swindon; Willenhall and Wolverhampton.

Six NGRC Permit Racecourses are: Henlow, Ipswich, Long Eaton, Norton, Canes, Rye House and Yarmouth.

Grooming: (*see* Fig. 6) A greyhound should be groomed every day with a brush and gloves. The old-fashioned horse-hair gloves are not made now, but there is a very good substitute supplied by H. J. Porter (Greyhounds) Ltd, of Hendon (advertising in the *Greyhound Magazine* and the *Greyhound Owner*). An old silk scarf to finally polish the coat will remove any loose hair. A good alternative is to buy a piece of velvet and make two 'gloves' or bags to fit the hands, with a hole each side towards the top to slip the thumb through (they can then be used for either hand). These last for a long time as they can be washed.

A hack-saw blade, used in the same way as a comb, is perfect for summer grooming when it is ideal for gently removing the undercoat.

Growth: A greyhound, apart from generally maturing and developing muscles, etc., is fully grown by the time he reaches the age of ten months.

Guarding the Racing Greyhound: All the care and attention given to the racing greyhound during training will count for nothing unless he is guarded *night and day* during periods when he is racing. Few, if any, establishments housing racing animals in England are free from outside interference – unless it already comes from inside.

Large airy kennels, with spacious grounds and paddocks, may rightly be described as the 'greyhounds' paradise' – and also the 'doper's playground'! If you have a kennel housing other people's dogs and you have

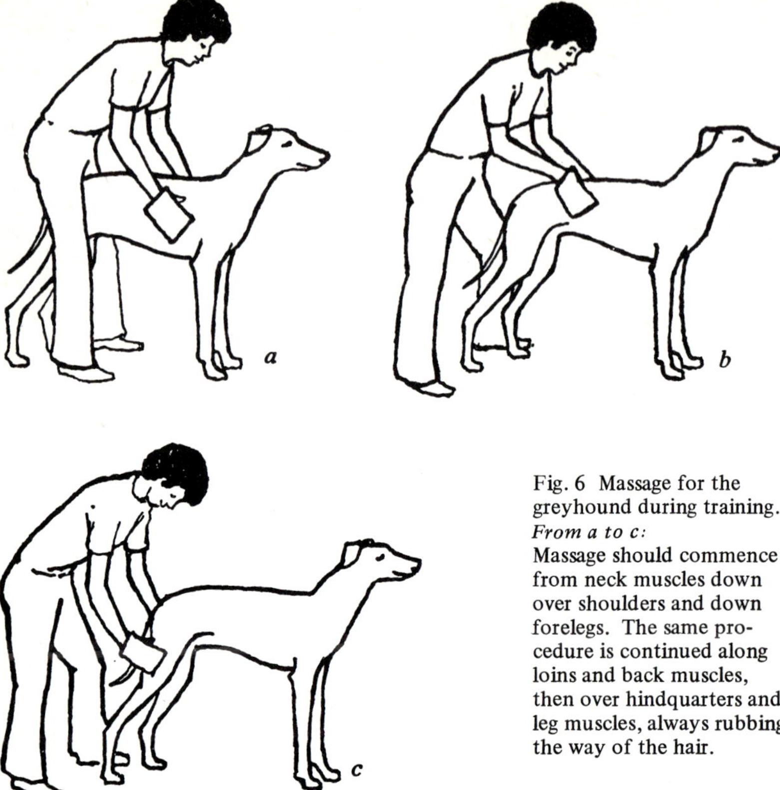

Fig. 6 Massage for the greyhound during training. *From a to c:* Massage should commence from neck muscles down over shoulders and down forelegs. The same procedure is continued along loins and back muscles, then over hindquarters and leg muscles, always rubbing the way of the hair.

any greyhounds in training for racing be suspicious of all owners. This is the only way as you will then soon be able to detect the owner only there for access to the kennels. Unfortunately, he will at first appear to be just as good an owner as the genuine one. His bills will be paid almost before they are due and his references will be so good that you may not delve into them. He will go to great lengths to explain what good owners he and his wife are – for she always has to come into it – the wonderful things they will do for their dogs on retirement, etc., etc. Liars need good memories, and it won't be long before this owner says something during conversation which will cast doubts on all these statements. No one who can give a substance or drug to a dog, which will cause blindness when he runs hard, may possibly kill him and, at the very least, cause him to finish lame or injured, can have affection for any animal. So be suspicious; the genuine owner doesn't have to keep telling you of all the good things he will do for his dog for it isn't in his nature to do otherwise.

There is no doubt that organized crime is on the increase throughout the world and gambling has always been a prime target. Since the advent of betting shops it must be much easier for the small-time crook to make money, if he can be certain that animals have no chance of winning their races. However, many of these shops are now being taken over by the big Turf Accountants which should help the racing world, for the fewer hands the money goes through the easier it must be to trace malpractices.

The easiest way to 'get at' dogs, with the least chance of being quickly found out, is by planting an employee in the kennels. He, or she, will be a good worker – up early and late to bed and always wanting to be 'on the job'. You won't be suspicious if you find him, or her, where you possibly didn't expect to. If, and when, you have removed this menace from your kennels, don't think this will be the end of it. The organizers – through one of their willing recruits – will still persist and it won't be safe to leave a kennel door or window open, or a dog loose in a paddock, even for a moment. Unfortunately, the greyhound is a great lover of titbits and that is all he will think he is receiving, for anything offered will be well camouflaged.

For some time the stadiums' kennels where dogs were placed, for anything up to four hours prior to racing, tended to be insecure. It was, and still is, an NGRC rule that each greyhound, after being examined by the veterinary surgeon and the stewards, had to be placed in an allotted kennel until his race.

It was allowed, and by Wimbledon Stadium encouraged, that the kennel should be thoroughly searched by the kennel-hand in charge of the dog, as the kennels were unguarded until each race meeting. Once the kennels had been searched and the doors locked, it was found there were *only two* ranges of these kennels where the dogs were completely safe from outside interference. These were the kennel ranges of Wimbledon and Southend stadiums. As these were under the same management, presumably they were constructed by the same builder and were all similar, with flush walls and doors. Once the door was closed, there was no opening except a high window to each kennel – sloping inwards – over a glass verandah which ran above the kennel doors. All the other ranges were insecure in that they had sliding windows or shutters, gaps along the outside tops of doors, peep-holes, trap doors which could be opened from the front, and many kennels connected from the inside with large gaps between each one.

There are paddock stewards, and they do a good job, but with over fifty kennels in a paddock, and people coming and going with dogs, they cannot keep their eyes on everything – and should not have to try. It is always advisable to muzzle a dog when placing him in the racing kennel, but before doing so, sweep out or thoroughly wipe out the kennel. Then stand outside the kennel and see that this isn't opened.

Guarding Owners: Under National Greyhound Racing Club rules, it is the practice to 'guard' owners should they have more than one entry registered in their name, in a stakes comprising more than one race (as heats and final). This can mean that the draw for traps is not really a true 'draw' at all.

In the 1940s, the late Fred Trevillion had six entries in the Greyhound Derby (eight heats of six dogs). Under this rule, his dogs had to be infiltrated through the draw, so that he didn't have more than one runner in any heat. At the Derby luncheon, there was an owner whose entry had not come out of the drum when only the last seven were left to be drawn. Longing for his dog to draw the last trap in the seventh heat, he had no chance of this for there were two of Trevillion's dogs still to be placed, so one had to go in each heat.

Even had the six dogs been drawn with the others, and found themselves all in one heat, the owner would have been certain of three qualifying for the next round – which would have been a very good average.

Hard Pad: (*see* DISTEMPER and HARD PAD).

Heart Disease: Not particularly common in greyhounds.

Heat: (*see* OESTRUM).

Hepatitis and Leptospirosis: A disease of the liver. Either disease, as well as a high temperature, may show symptoms of jaundice – where the whites of the eyes and the gums are tinged with varying degrees of yellow. These, together with distemper and hard pad, are the scourge of the canine world. They are all virus diseases and are known as 'killer' diseases, as they so often prove fatal.

They are said to be spread by a dog coming into contact with the urine of a rat and passing the virus to other canines.

Puppies can be inoculated against both diseases, as well as older dogs, and your vet should be consulted.

Holland: In Holland greyhound racing is run on Club lines. Impallah, the Dutch champion of the 1960s, was a winner of thirty-five races, including the European Championship, in three successive years – 1962, 1963 and 1964.

Bred from English stock, Impallah had two of England's Derby winners in her pedigree; her sire was Extra Gun, a son of Ballylanigan Tanist, who won the Derby in 1951, while the 1949 winner, Narrogar Ann, was her great-grand-dam.

Identification: A dog must wear a collar in public places with the name and address of the owner inscribed on the collar or on a plate or badge attached to the collar.

Identity Book: This is really the greyhound's passport, for he cannot take part in trial or race unless it is in the possession of the racing manager of the track he attends. After each trial or race all information and statistics have to be entered on the book by the manager or his assistant. Before taking part in a trial or race he has to be checked against the Identity Book for colour, markings, weight, etc. (*See* WEIGHT.)

In-Breeding: This is mating a bitch to a close relation to intensify the good points and characteristics required. It may, however, intensify the bad points of the family.

Independent Tracks: Licensed for greyhound racing by local councils – but not for racing under National Greyhound Racing Club rules.

Three of these tracks have quite recently joined the NGRC and will race under their rules. The tracks are Cambridge, Ipswich and Rye House (Hertfordshire). Dogs racing at these tracks will now have Identity Books issued by the NGRC in which all performances, whether trials or races, will be entered. This book is kept by the NGRC and forwarded by them, on request from a track official, when a dog is due to race or have a trial at this track. The owner of the dog does not have charge of this book.

Each track has to be brought up to the standard required, including facilities for patrons, etc., but, formerly, even when the track did meet with all requirements, they were often kept apart because of the different ruling on the kennelling of greyhounds prior to racing.

Whereas under NGRC rules a dog had to be placed in his racing kennel for up to five hours before he raced, the dog at the independent track was accepted ten minutes before he raced. This rule has now been adjusted and independent tracks joining the NGRC will be allowed to accept dogs half-an-hour before they race. This would be a very welcome rule for all greyhound racing tracks – for many a race has been lost through a 'kennel-fretter' being kennelled for so long that he had expended most of his energy before reaching the race-track.

The Provincial Greyhound Tracks, the old association incorporating the independent tracks, has now been renamed The Provincial Tracks Federation, and affiliated with the NGRC.

Inoculation: It was in the 1950s when, thanks to years of unceasing research, the scourge of distemper and hard pad showed real signs of being brought to a halt. It was then that this vicious killer, which had claimed the lives of so many dogs, found that it was losing its grip against the new vaccine.

At this time, people were having their greyhound litters inoculated against distemper and hard pad when they were still in the nest and, often, only a few days old. However, it is best to leave it until they are a few months old since inoculations at this age give a much better protection. It was noticed that those puppies inoculated in the nest showed a nervous trait even though they had not been bred from nervous stock. In greyhound racing, this is a great drawback.

Since those days, still further progress has been made in ensuring that a safe and effective vaccine is produced for inoculation. Canilep-DDX is what Glaxo Laboratories called the 'great protector'. Coming from their veterinary laboratories, your vet will supply this and inoculate your dog, giving him protection from distemper/hard pad and hepatitis and leptospirosis. You should not let your dog walk outside your own yards or kennels until he has been inoculated.

Booster doses for adult dogs are recommended by Glaxo in the prevention of distemper (which induces hard pad), canine virus hepatitis, leptospirosis canicola and leptospirosis icterohaemorrhagiae.

Glaxo state: 'All these are extremely serious diseases for which there is no such treatment. Prevention is therefore all the more important. A particularly distressing feature is that they often cause damage in puppies which does not become apparent until later in their life.

'Because no vaccine, animal or human, can be guaranteed to give 100 per cent permanent protection, it is a good idea to give your dog regular reinforcing "booster" doses of vaccine. Your vet will possibly recommend a "booster" every year, but his advice will depend on his knowledge of local conditions and you should consult him about this when your dog is a year old. A "booster" is also a wise precaution when your dog is travelling to a new area, because any one of the diseases, though comparatively rare at home, may be a serious threat in the new neighbourhood.

Ireland: The governing body controlling racing in Ireland is the Irish Greyhound Racing Board in Limerick. There are racing tracks at Celtic Park, Clonmel, Cork, Dundalk, Enniscorthy, Galway, Harolds Cross, Kilkenny, Lifford, Limerick, Longford, Mullingar, Navan, Newbridge, Shelbourne Park, Thurles, Tralee, Waterford and Youghal.

Greyhounds entered in the Irish Greyhound Stud Book are also registered with the National Coursing Club. (*See* REGISTRATION.)

Ireland, 1979: Nameless Pixie (Bk bitch 1977) was voted Ireland's Racing Greyhound of the Year by a panel of Irish pressmen. This bitch, winner of the Irish Oaks and the 525 Carroll's International, was also third in both the Irish Greyhound Derby and the St Leger. Her sire was Monalee Champion and her dam was Itsastar. Owned by Mrs Rita McCauley, Nameless Pixie was bred by her husband Ben. This was her trainer's fourth National Award. The well-known Ger McKenna also trained the winners in 1967, 1969 and 1975.

So Careful was chosen as Ireland's Coursing Greyhound of the 1979/80 season, by a panel of judges. The black dog, a son of Careful Pat, is owned by Michael Daly of Tralee, and bred by Bridget McAuliffe, of Banard, Abbeyfeale. Trained by Brendan and Pa Fitzgerald. So Careful won the Harty Cup, at Abbeydorney; the Treaty Cup, at Limerick City; the Munster Cup at Newcastlewest; and the Champion Stakes at Powerstown Park. During the 1979/80 season this dog raised 27 flags in 30 courses and has a career record of 41 flags from 48 courses.

Irish Grand National, 1979: Run at Thurles Stadium, over the 525 yards hurdles course, the final was won by Keeragh Sambo (Bd dog 1975). His sire was Own Pride and his dam, Keeragh Flo. Time of race: 30.20 secs. Owned by Mr W. E. Read.

Irish Greyhound Derby: Sponsored by Messrs P. J. Carroll and Co. Ltd. In 1979 and 1980 the final of this race was run at Shelbourne Park Stadium over a distance of 525 yards.

In 1979 the winner was Penny County (F bitch March 1977). Sire: Dark Mercury; Dam: Columbcille Aim. Time of race: 20.28 secs. First prize: £20,000. Owners: Messrs S. Dunne and F. Hurney of Co. Dublin.

In 1980 the winner was Suir Miller (Bd dog August 1978). Sire: Minnesota Miller; Dam: Mor Cream. Time of race: 29.18 secs. First prize: £22,500. Trainer: Michael Barrat.

Irish Laurels, 1979: Sponsored by Cashman and run at Cork Stadium over 525 yards flat the final was won by Knockrour Slave (W & Bk dog April 1977). Sire: Sole Aim; Dam: Knockrour Exile. Time of race: 20.45 secs. Owner: Mr D. Lynch, of Aghabullogue, received the £6,000 and trophy.

Ireland's Major Open Race Winners – 1979

Event	*Winner*	*Distance (yards)*	*Track*	*Owner*	*Prize Money*
Carroll's Irish Derby	Penny County	525	Shelbourne Park	Ms Dunne & P. Hurney	£20,000
The Lyon Industrial Estate Oaks	Nameless Pixie Knockrour	525	Harold's Cross	Mrs Rita McCauley	10,000
Cashman Irish Laurels	Knockrour Slave	525	Cork	Mr D. Lynch	6,000
Smithwick's Irish St. Leger	Airmount Champ	550	Limerick	Mr A Kiely	6,000
National Breeders' Produce Stakes	Hune Highway	525	Clonmel	Miss P. McGrath	4,000
Burmah-Castrol Puppy Derby	Tivoli Can't	525	Harold's Cross	M. O'Toole	4,000
Sunday World Leger	Corlecky Glory	575	Shelbourne Park	Mr M. Bruton	3,600
Guinness '600'	Tough Decision	600	Shelbourne Park	Mr H. McLemon & R. Barber	3,500
Respond Champion Stakes	Distant Clamour	525	Shelbourne Park	Mr J. Hogarty	3,500
The Carroll's 525 International	Nameless Pixie	525	Dundalk	Mrs R. McAuley	3,000
Bloom 550	Orange Prince	550	Tralee	Mrs M. Kenny	3,000

Jaundice: Although the dog will already have shown signs of being off-colour, such as dullness and loss of appetite, it is not until the eyes and lips show a distinct tinge of yellow that jaundice is confirmed. Later the skin of the hairless parts of the body will also turn yellow. Usually there is constipation and what is passed from the bowel will be grey or slate coloured. Jaundice means that the liver is not functioning properly and the bile is being deposited in the tissues of the body instead of being secreted in the liver.

Obstructive jaundice is caused by gall-stones (worms by way of the bile duct) or a catarrhal condition or stricture of the duct, or by growths on the liver or pancreas causing pressure on the duct.

Non-obstructive jaundice is caused by congestion of the liver, destruction of the liver cells or toxic agents in the blood, as in distemper or some form of poisoning. Your vet should be called in.

Jealousy: There is no dog more jealous than the greyhound, and jealousy is one of his most important attributes. It is only this which causes one dog to race faster than another to obtain – or have first refusal of – the prize in front.

Without jealousy the greyhound would not persevere, and it is when this quality is lacking that a dog, racing or coursing, is termed dodgy or 'un-genuine'. This may mean anything from slowing, baulking or trying to stop his opponent from running out his race. A dog can only concentrate on one thing at a time and – without jealousy – he just does not concentrate enough.

Just before the Second World War, cheetahs were brought to England, with a view to racing them. Termed the 'fastest living creatures', they were to chase meat in their races. But as they are not jealous creatures, and as there were no public cheetah races I presume they did not prove satisfactory.

Very often, the breeder or handler is blamed for a greyhound having no jealousy because he or she has 'spoilt' the dog. This isn't true, because any living thing must become attached to that which feeds him. The puppy likely to be short of jealousy can often be detected when only a few weeks old; never wanting to be first to anything and always waiting behind to see the human being. When selecting a dog or bitch for breeding, this is the trait to be avoided at all costs if the stock is wanted for racing or coursing.

Kennel Club: Formed in 1873, this is a vast organization at 1 Clarges Street, London W1Y 8AB, which covers all aspects of the breeding and showing of pedigree dogs registered under its rules.

Kennel Club Gazette: Published by the Kennel Club, this gives all necessary information regarding forthcoming shows.
Kennel Club Stud Book: This is published yearly.

Lactation, Defective: A very small supply or complete suppression of the secretion of milk. The milk glands should be stimulated by gentle massage. The diet should be of raw meat, and the bitch should also be encouraged to take plenty of gruel made from fine oatmeal, or Robinson's Groats, as directed. There is also a Lactol product on the market which is very effective in the treatment of this trouble.

Lactation, Excessive: When the glands are swollen, hard and painful through the secretion of too much milk which often dribbles away. It may occur with a maiden bitch having a large secretion of milk, which will show itself seven or eight weeks after heat. The bitch appears very restless and miserable. She always appears to look for puppies and will often scratch and rake at her bed, then twist round and round as though making a nest. In the case of a maiden bitch in milk she may be given a purgative medicine, such as castor oil, once or twice a week (but only if you *know* she has not been pregnant). Unless the milk collects in such large quantities that it is painful for her, it is better not to draw this off as it will increase the supply of milk. The glands may be dabbed with a lotion made from one pint of tepid water to which has been added three tablespoonfuls of gin (harmless if licked, but pleasant!).

It is essential that a maiden bitch is treated when in this condition, otherwise the milk can curdle and become hard – this could cause the start of mammary tumours (*see* TUMOURS). The diet should contain no meat and food should be given dry, with water to drink.

Excessive lactation may occur in pregnant bitches, just before or after the puppies are born. In this case, gently draw off a little of the milk, night and morning. Do *not* give any purgative medicine and do not put anything on the glands, as the puppies may be put off their feed. I have never known a greyhound bitch, with puppies, where they couldn't deal with any excess milk the mother may have. If she has lost all her puppies, she should be treated as specified for a maiden bitch.

Laxatives: Use Dinneford's Fluid Magnesia for young puppies and Epsom Salts for saplings and grown dogs.

Lead Poisoning: (*see* POISONS, LEAD).

Leptospirosis: (*see* HEPATITIS).

Licensing: Every person who keeps a dog over the age of six months must obtain a licence from the Post Office, which is renewable every twelve months. The only exemptions from licensing a dog are: (1) dogs under six months of age; (2) dogs for the blind; (3) dogs kept for working cattle or sheep and (4) foxhounds.

Life, Termination of: Life is a time when it is hoped that the greyhound receives from his 'keeper' the care and affection on which he thrives. As with all living things, discipline is necessary during his rearing, but let this be tempered with kindness and he will be the companion to man he was destined to be. Unfortunately his life – which even in health is far too short – sometimes has to be terminated. When he suffers incurable pain or when through some affliction he is too old or infirm to enjoy his life, then it is time to call in your vet and let him be 'put to sleep' painlessly. Do not send him away, but let this be done in the place he has known as home.

Mammary (or Milk) Glands: These occur both in the male and female of all mammals. In the male they are imperfectly developed; so the secretory power is limited to the females to nourish their young. (*See* LACTATION, EXCESSIVE and TUMOURS.)

Mange, Follicular: This is a skin disease more often confined to puppies and young dogs, although adult dogs do contract it and may carry it all their lives. As the disease is hereditary, bitches may pass it on to their young. It is fairly easily contracted when dogs are living together, but not so easily through casually meeting. A progressive disease, mange will start with a small patch on the body or legs, as do so many other skin troubles; but in follicular mange the patch is a dirty grey in colour, with fairly large pimples or pustules containing fluid or pus in which the parasites are found. Often incurable, this is very difficult to treat, and your vet should be called immediately. Follicular mange is not contagious to human beings.

Mange, Sarcoptic: A parasitic and contagious skin disease and caused by a parasite which can only be seen under a microscope. When sarcoptic mange is suspected, a scraping of skin must be taken from one of the patches, and sent for diagnosis. The disease is contagious and is easily spread through the use of brushes, blankets, baskets, coats and kennels. It is also contagious to human beings and is then called scabies. Rats, mice and cats are also subject to the disease, and are often the cause of the infection.

There is great irritation as the parasite burrows under the skin, causing bare patches, sores and injuries to the skin which dry and form into scabs. The dog scratches incessantly and loses condition. This mange is easily cured and, by prompt treatment, is soon made free from contagion. The main ingredient in the treatment of mange is, and always has been, sulphur. Either flowers of sulphur or black sulphur; one part sulphur to nine parts of olive oil, almond oil or vaseline. This mixture should be rubbed well over the dog every four days, three times a day. Four days after the last application the dog should be washed in a mild shampoo – or with a gentle soap. It is important to fumigate thoroughly the kennels which have housed dogs suffering from mange. This may be done with a formalin candle, bought from any chemist or druggist, or by scrubbing the kennel out thoroughly with strong Jeyes Fluid diluted in water. The kennel must be left open for all fumes to disappear before the dog is allowed to return to it. Brushes, coats, etc., must be washed in a disinfectant solution, and leads and collars should be left in the kennel whilst fumigation is carried out.

Mastitis (Inflammation of the Breast): A complaint not uncommon in bitches when they are nursing their puppies. Usually septic, the infection comes through a split or crack in the nipple of the breast, sometimes through a blind teat. One or more of the milk glands may be affected.

Symptoms: The bitch usually goes off her feed, for the breast is swollen and tender and there is fever and a good deal of pain. A saline purge, such as Milk of Magnesia, and hot fomentations on the swelling will help to prevent an abscess forming.

The bitch's milk needs to be drawn off at regular intervals by the puppies, by manipulation or a breast-pump.

Your vet should be called immediately because, apart from other necessary treatment he may recommend, if only one gland is affected, he may be able to bandage this successfully so that the puppies may use the other teats.

Mating: It is usual for the bitch to be taken to the dog for service, between the thirteenth and eighteenth day from when she came 'in season'. This is calculated from the very first day the bitch shows colour from the vulva (entrance to the vagina). The colour may at first be slight, but will increase as the vulva swells. The day of mating may vary depending on the age of the bitch, whether it is a first litter, etc. When booking the mating the owner or stud groom of the dog will give advice. (*See* COPULATION.)

Milk:

Analysis of cows' and the stronger bitches milk:

	Cows	*Bitches*
Water	87.4	66.3
Fats	4.0	14.8
Sugar and Soluble Salts	5.0	2.9
Casein and Insoluble Salts	3.6	16.0
	100.0%	100.0%

Monorchidism: Where only one of the dog's testicles descends into the scrotum. A serious fault in the show greyhound as it would not be accepted in the show ring. It would make no difference as regards coursing or racing but, although the dog is able to reproduce, the fault is hereditary and may be passed on to his progeny.

Muriatic Acid: The old name of Hydrochloric Acid. (*See* BREAD.)

Muscles, Pulled or Torn: Very common among racing greyhounds. Racing at speed on bad going, turning on bends, especially on a track where rain has fallen on a former hard surface and made the going slippery, are some of the causes. As with a broken hock, the dog seldom finds his former speed again – even if the muscles appear to heal – but a lot depends on the degree of injury, which can be varied.

Symptoms: An injured shoulder muscle seems to have a better chance of recovery than one in a hind leg; there is always a swelling with bad bruising. Although the bruising shows at the seat of the injury, the swelling is usually lower as the fluid and blood find the lowest point of the leg. Apart from walking on the lead, rest is essential until the swelling has completely gone, and the dog must be kept from racing or galloping for a long time.

There are advanced treatments for muscle trouble. One means surgery whereby the muscle is cut and, after the operation, stitched up again. A qualified veterinary surgeon will do this, or he may take the dog to the Royal Veterinary College where an expert team take over.

Four dogs, of which I had charge, were operated on at the college. The operations were successful in that the muscles healed so that the dogs had no trouble whilst taking ordinary exercise but, although two of them had been top-class open racers, none of them ever reached form which justified their being kept as racers. The other two did race again and won one or two very low-class graded races.

Muzzles: Every greyhound must wear a muzzle whilst racing. The best one is the one approved by the NGRC (*see* Fig. 7).

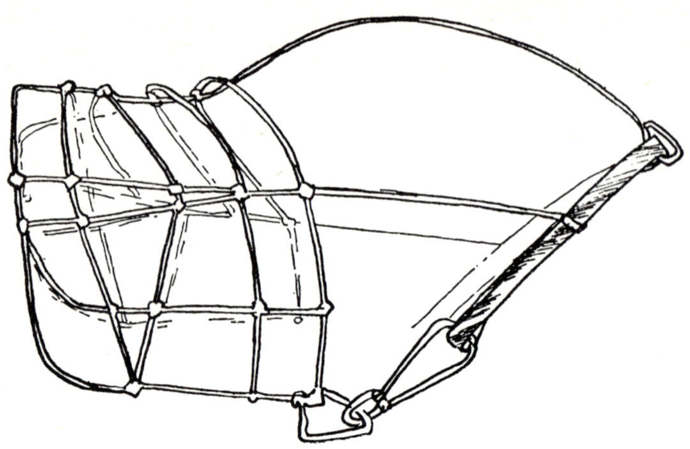

Fig. 7 Racing muzzle as approved by the NGRC

It is sometimes necessary to muzzle the bitch during mating so that she does not turn and snap at the dog. Dogs should also be muzzled whilst travelling by train. (*See* BOX MUZZLE.)

National Coursing Club: 35/37 Grosvenor Gardens, London, SW1. This organization is run on the same lines as the Jockey Club and members are elected. They issue an annual *Stud Book*. (*See* REGISTRATION and 'STONEHENGE'.)

National Greyhound Racing Club Ltd: The Club was formed in 1928 as the controlling body for the conduct and well-being of greyhound racing in England, Scotland and Wales. It became an incorporated body in 1972 and the code of rules, drawn up originally in 1928, was continued.

Address: The National Greyhound Racing Club Ltd, 24/28 Oval Road, London, NW1 7DA.

Rules include: The registration of all greyhounds racing on courses approved by the Club. All possible steps to be taken for the checking of the correct identity of greyhounds running on these racecourses. Investigating all reports of improper practices and breaches of Rules by owners, trainers, officials and others. To take disciplinary action against those found guilty, either by warning them off all licensed and approved racecourses or by imposing fines – or by other methods. To license all racecourses and all officials engaged on racecourses, also racecourse trainers and their staff. To license all private trainers and their staff. Each licence issued to have the photograph of its owner displayed on the licence. Veterinary supervision at all race meetings and stadium kennels where greyhounds are housed. All kennels periodically inspected by the Club's stewards to check condition of kennels and well-being of the greyhounds there and the number of inmates checked. A Trainer's report to be sent each month to the NGRC, stating number of dogs in kennels, reporting sickness, etc., and each report to be accompanied by a certificate signed by a veterinary surgeon and stating condition of dogs.

The NGRC Ltd publish as an official record the *National Greyhound Racing Calendar*, containing the official announcements of the Stewards and a list of officials licensed. Also the conditions, entries and results of all Open Races (this is issued fortnightly – by subscription – and can be obtained from the above address).

Since its inception the NGRC has given good service to British greyhound racing. Through the high standards required under Club rules, racegoers can enjoy a well-organized sport under favourable conditions.

Much of the help and supervision given to the main participant – the greyhound – may not be obvious to the racing public. NGRC stewards pay unannounced visits to all kennels and establishments where greyhounds are kept under licences issued to private and track trainers. If the dogs are not found to be adequately housed and cared for the trainer's licence will be withdrawn.

See also RETIRED GREYHOUND TRUST, THE *(page 107).*

National Greyhound Racing Society of Great Britain Ltd: An association of companies owning racecourses, licensed by the National Greyhound Racing Club, to race under its rules. The body deals with legal and administrative matters affecting the sport and is recognized by Departments of State and local governing authorities.

Nephritis: Inflammation of the kidneys, usually caused by a severe chill or stone in the kidneys. *Symptoms:* sudden attack of shivering with a rise in temperature, up to three or four degrees, with a rapid pulse. Pain in back; vomiting; scanty and high-coloured urine, or blood may be mixed with water. If suppressed, the dog may suffer from uraemic poisoning. Call vet who may arrange for X-rays for diagnosis.

Nursing: This is a very important item as so often it is the attention given during illness which saves a patient's life. First of all, if kept in the house, the sick greyhound needs a well-ventilated room with plenty of light, dry and free from draughts and the temperature of the room kept to 60°F. If it is summer and hot, the window should be opened (fresh air has never killed; it is the foul air which sometimes does). Any carpet should be taken up and a thick layer of newspaper spread all over the floor. This is a convenient form of bedding since it is easily changed.

If living outside, the dog still needs a warm and comfortable kennel – 60°F. free from draughts, etc. Thick newspaper should again be put on the floor, as it helps to soak up any wetness. The patient should not be allowed out of the room or kennel until he has recovered and his temperature is back to normal, unless it is on the advice of your vet. The dog and the kennel must be kept scrupulously clean. The smell of ammonia is very harmful to an ill dog and can cause damage to the eyes. The sick dog needs his mouth wiped with a soft cloth soaked and wrung out in a very weak solution of warm water and TCP or any other mild disinfectant which does *not* contain carbolic. Keep the eyes free of discharge with a little weak solution of warm water and boracic powder. Optrex may be used instead. Clean the teeth and the inside of the mouth with a very weak solution of warm water and permanganate of potash (when the water has turned pink after the addition of the crystals).

If sickness of any sort is suspected in the kennels, provide at once a bucket of strong disinfectant – Jeyes Fluid is good for this – and wear boots which have been plunged into the bucket before walking through to the separate kennels. Shake all the surplus fluid from the boots after taking them out of the bucket and before going into the kennels. Every food bowl, after being washed in the usual way, should be 'baked' in the oven until all germs have been destroyed. This is where the 'Bithel' bowl comes to be so useful, as it seems to withstand any harsh treatment. First made some years ago by the owner of the greyhound Model Dasher, the bowl became almost as famous as the dog (*see* BITHEL BOWL).

When feeding sick dogs the diet and preparation of the food is most important – a reliable person should be responsible for this.

All milk food should be freshly made. Feeding should be little and often, as a dog will recover far more quickly if he takes the food voluntarily rather than having to be fed. Benger's Food, Slippery Elm Food, Farex, Robinson's Groats or similar foods made with milk into a gruel are very nourishing, but so often a sick dog will refuse milky foods, and then needs to be tempted with something else. Scraped raw meat may be given, but in small quantities. A good beef tea, made with about half a pound of beef cut into small pieces and a pint of water added, simmered in an oven for two or three hours, is very nourishing. Do not feed the meat but give the concentrated gravy warm or cold. This 'tea' may be varied by using veal, lamb or rabbit. Also, fish steamed in a little milk or water is good. If the dog's bowels are relaxed, some rice may be added and simmered with any of these foods, but it will be necessary to allow a little more water in the cooking. Sheep's brains, boiled in a little milk, are good for the invalid; also calves' sweetbreads. These foods may be more readily accepted than the milk foods. Brand's Essence (beef or chicken) is another nourishing food helpful in the care of invalid dogs. If the dog is taking only a little food at a time, it is advisable to give him some during the night as well as the day.

Unless you have other instructions from your vet, fresh water should always be left with the dog, but this should first be boiled and then allowed to get cold.

The dog should be coated. This can easily be done with a jacket made of flannel or something similar. Alternatively, the ordinary greyhound coat, or rug, may be used but it may be necessary to give some extra warmth under and around the stomach as well. A small or medium sized woman's woollen jumper is ideal for this – preferably one with short sleeves. Through the neck and hem of the jumper run a piece of elastic to make the jumper just close enough to be cosy but not too tight.

The dog's temperature should be taken night and morning, and a note made of this (*see* TEMPERATURE). The dog's pulse is sometimes a better guide to his health and if this is slow and 'thready' it is more serious than a fast but regular pulse. The heartbeat of a dog – unlike that of a human being – is intermittent and irregular. (*See* DOSING and PULSE.)

Oestrum or Heat: This is the period of menstruation in the bitch. In the greyhound it may not occur for the first time until she is between nine and twelve months old – or even later. It may then occur regularly twice a year – or again, not quite so frequently in the greyhound bitch.

It is recognized by the vulva swelling and a slight mucous discharge continuing for about a week when the discharge is pinkish. In a few days this becomes blood-coloured. The heat lasts from three to four weeks from commencement to the end, but the bitch should not be put back with a dog (unless, of course, you are going to breed from her) for at least thirty days from the first day of the heat.

'One Thousand Guineas': This is a classic race and was first promoted by London Stadiums, when it was always run at Park Royal Stadium over

400 yards. Since the closure of this group of tracks the race has been run at Hackney Stadium over 330 yards.

The 1979 final was won by Ashmore Fun (Bd dog by Monalee Champion and Shady Raffle). Time: 29.64 secs over a distance of 484 metres. Owner: Mr D. Morris. Trainer: D. Vass. Race sponsored by Mecca Bookmakers.

Open Kennel System: One way to combat the menace of infiltration into racing establishments by 'undesirables' is to cut to a minimum the number of people having access to greyhounds during rearing, training and racing.

The open kennel system, used in the very successful promoting of greyhound racing in Australia – and also in Ireland – is not used under the NGRC rules of racing in England. The nearest to this is the granting of a licence by the NGRC whereby an owner may privately train his own dogs and those of his immediate family. This licence may also be extended so that the training of other people's greyhounds may be carried on from a private kennel. Great strides have also been made with the introduction of contract training, under NGRC rules (*see* CONTRACT TRAINING).

The greyhound tracks licensed to race by local councils – but not under NGRC rules – only race greyhounds under the open kennel system. This means that the dogs are at all times in the care of their owners. Whilst the markings of the dogs are taken for identification, there is no extensive system of registration, either with the National Coursing Club or by the National Greyhound Racing Club. These council tracks do not offer the facilities of those governed by the NGRC, nor anything approaching the same scale of prize money. Therefore, the main attraction can only be that the owners of these dogs may have sole charge of them all the time. The greyhounds are presented for racing only ten minutes before they have to run in their race and they are kennelled before racing only from choice. Yet the dogs are seldom late, which would mean their withdrawal from the race. Dogs at one time used to be kept waiting in stadium kennels from four to five hours before they raced, often fretting most of the time and becoming over-excited prior to the race.

With present day difficulties of ever-changing staff, surely when greyhounds are put in stadium kennels, their handlers could have the option of going in with them or, alternatively, keeping them in their own vans until they are due to race? After being examined by the veterinary surgeon, could not the muzzles and coats be shown to be satisfactory by

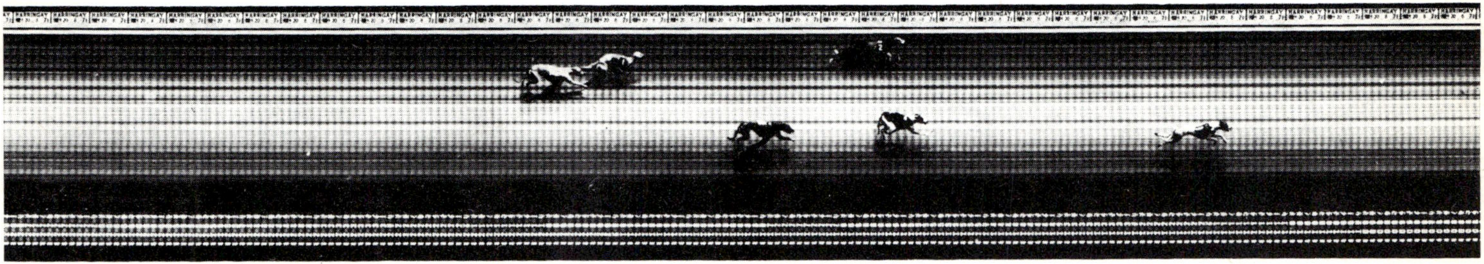

12. (*above*): The Photo-finish

13. Lure Tronic Device (*By permission of the Lure Tronic Co., USA*)

14. The Prince of Wales receiving Whisky and Soda on 19 November 1973 as his feudal dues as Duke of Cornwall (*By permission of the Western Morning News*)

15. Lacca Champion, the winner of Spiller Derby, White City, in 1978. Owned by Mrs S. Pearce (*By permission of the Greyhound Racing Association*)

the handler, with a steward watching? This would cut security measures by half since there would be far fewer people in contact with the racer. (*See* TEMPERATURE.)

Origin of the Greyhound: The origin of the dog still remains a mystery, but we know from sculpture found on Egyptian tombs of the Fourth Dynasty that a hunting dog of a greyhound type was used in Ancient Egypt. The Ancient Greeks too had a hound-type dog for hunting and, as their quarry was usually the hare, it is possible that the greyhound originated in Greece. It is not accepted that the name greyhound ever referred to the colour of the dog; one theory is that the name came from Grekhound (Greekhound). Another theory is that it originated from Gazehound, now in the dictionary as 'a hound that hunts by sight'. Last, but not least, it is believed that the name may derive from the Icelandic *greyhundr* (*grey* meaning dog, and *hundr* hound).

Whatever the origin of his name, the greyhound is the only dog to be mentioned in the Bible. Proverbs 30, verses 29-31: 'There be three things which go well, yea, four are comely in the going: A lion which is strongest among beasts, and turneth not away for any; A Greyhound; an he goat also; and a king, against whom there is no rising up.'

There is no doubt that greyhounds were in England from a very early date, but their numbers would have greatly increased with the coming of the Normans, who were great followers of the chase. At this time, many areas were laid waste and villages were even destroyed, to provide forest-land where the Normans could indulge in their favourite sport. One such well-known area is the New Forest in Hampshire.

Of all the dogs, the greyhound must be one of the highest on the list for his love of human beings, perhaps because he has always hunted with man. Very seldom is one of these dogs found to be spiteful or vicious, and then it can usually be traced to cruelty on the part of someone he has trusted.

The oft-times quoted lines from Wynkyn de Worde's *Treatise* of 1496 gives a good description of what a greyhound should be:

A greyhounde should be headed lyke a snake, and
Neckyed lyke a drake,
Fotyd lyke a cat,
Taylyd lyke a ratte,
Syded lyke a teme, and
Chyned lyke a bream.

Oscars, 1979: A panel of judges, from The Greyhound Trainers' Association and The Greyhound Breeders' Forum, voted two greyhounds as joint winners of the 1979 Silver Award. They were Geoff De Mulder's Desert Pilot and Tom Johnston's Kilmagoura Mist, who shared this Greyhound of the Year title.

Kilmagoura Mist won the Ladbroke's St Leger at Wembley, the Mann's Milton Keyneas Derby at Bletchley, and ran second in the Oaks at Harringay. With 11 wins from 31 races her prize money was over £12,000.

Desert Pilot had 16 wins from 24 races, with prize money of over £7,000. Winning the Skol Select Stakes and Summer Cup at Wembley, and the Wm Hill Nationwide Championship at White City, he was also third in the Greyhound Derby. The judges gave a special award to De Mulder's Sarah's Bunny, the 1979 Derby winner. She also won the Eclipse Stakes at Coventry, and was runner-up in Belle Vue's Northern Flat Championship. Her prize money exceeded £23,000. Paddy Milligan's Gay Flash was awarded the title of Best English-bred Greyhound for her victories in the Gold Collar at Catford, and the Coronation Stakes at Wembley. From 19 wins in 37 races, she earned over £7,000.

Weston Star, whose dam was also a Silver Award winner, took the Best English-bred Dam title for the prowess of her two litters. Her 1976 litter, by Westmead County, included BBC trophy winner, Weston Blaze, and, also, Weston Princess, Weston Sparrow and Weston Superstar. Her November 1977 litter, by Clear Reason, included Weston Whisky, winner of the Northern Puppy Cup at Owlerton, Weston Beauty and Weston Soda. Owners of these winners were presented with the coveted Silver Oscars at greyhound racing's Silver Ball, at The Hilton, London.

Out-Crossing: Breeding with completely unrelated sire and dam. If of good sound stock, this will often counteract faults which can be brought out through too much in-breeding – caused by the pursuit of winning sires and dams.

Out-crossing for colour may sometimes be necessary, as continuous breeding by mating fawn, and/or white, sires and dams will gradually produce puppies with coats becoming lighter and lighter. The progeny will not be impaired through the colour of their coats, but persistently mating fawn with fawn will also bring lighter eyes, which can be especially detrimental to the greyhound. Light eyes have not the good clear sight of dark eyes and the prowess and speed of top racing greyhounds are very closely linked with quick sightedness.

Over-Heating: (*see* SKIN IRRITATION).

Ovarid: A product from the Glaxo Laboratories, for the postponement of heat (or season) in a bitch. Helpful to the owner of the 'family' bitch when holidays are in the offing and for the bitch which may roam, bringing the heartaches and troubles of the unwanted litter.

Especially useful for the exhibition bitch with a show-date in mind, when she would be safe from being molested by other show-dogs, nor would she upset them.

Widely used in the racing world, where the greyhound bitch usually strikes peak form just before coming in season and, in the past, so often had to be withdrawn from the final of a big race to take this enforced rest.

The use – and safety – of Ovarid is best described in Glaxo's own words: 'Ovarid is a unique tablet containing magestrol acetate for the suppression or postponement of "heat". The active ingredient is used in a well-known and successful human "pill".'

Glaxo has taken great pains to ensure that Ovarid is safe and reliable in its effect on bitches, provided it is administered correctly. Starting in 1962, exhaustive tests on many breeds have been carried out to make sure that Ovarid not only works, but works safely. The evidence of these tests is supported by pracitcal experience over a number of years with a similar product in Finland.

When to use Ovarid: Start the bitch on an eight-day course of Ovarid tablets when 'heat' is confirmed by vaginal swelling and discharge. In the normal bitch these signs will have disappeared in about four days, male dogs will lose interest in the bitch and she will cease to be so excitable. Even if she is mated, the contraceptive effect of Ovarid can normally be relied upon provided that the dosage has been given for at least two complete days.

Ovarid works best in bitches with normal, regular 'heats'; for this reason it may be unwise to treat bitches at their first season. It should also be recognized that bitches showing abnormalities in their breeding cycle may not be good subjects. You should ask your veterinary surgeon to advise you on this and follow his instructions. To stop your bitch having puppies, there is no need to send her to kennels during 'heat', nor to resort to the irreversible expedient of having her spayed. An eight-day course of Ovarid tablets is the modern answer. Most bitches come on 'heat' again four to six weeks earlier than would normally have been expected had Ovarid not been given. This time you may wish to breed from your bitch. Alternatively, Ovarid may again be used to suppress 'heat'.

Ovarid can postpone 'heat' as well as suppress it once it has begun, if this is necessary. If you start giving your bitch Ovarid fourteen days before the journey, holiday, show or any other occasion you wish to cover, you can be sure that the problem of 'heat' will not trouble you. As long as the course continues, 'heat' will not occur (but no course should last more than forty days). Once the course is discontinued the breeding cycle will resume normally, but it is not possible to say with any accuracy when the next 'heat' will occur. It is possible that 'heat' will recur fairly soon after the end of the course but the usual time is two to three months later. It is unlikely to be delayed by more than six months.

With regard to the use of Ovarid to avoid the inconvenience of 'heat', Glaxo strongly recommend you to discuss this with your veterinary surgeon, for the timing of administering Ovarid is quite critical. Your vet can supply this product.

Over-work: It is very inadvisable to over-work your dogs. A quote from *The Courser's Guide* (1896) says: 'Horse exercise, or running behind a cart or trap, I do not approve of except occasionally, as, although perhaps you get the dogs to all appearance in good condition, with plenty of good hard muscle, they will generally be found to be troubled with the "slows". I saw an instance of this once at Four Oaks Park, where a gentleman had trained three greyhounds by constant work behind his phaeton, and when they were slipped they could scarcely go fast enough to keep themselves warm.'

Parturient Eclampsia: This occurs in excitable and nervous bitches two or three weeks after whelping. It is very rare in greyhound bitches.

The bitch, usually unable to stand, generally lies on her side with her legs stretched out, frothing at the mouth and panting. This distressing attack often lasts some hours, leaving the bitch exhausted. Although eclampsia seldom proves fatal, the bitch may have another attack after a few days. Examine the mammary glands and keep them empty until symptoms cease (*see* MASTITIS). Give a saline purge and avoid meat in her diet. She may have plenty of milk food, fish and tripe. Call your vet.

Perfect Greyhound, description of: As given in the *Book of St Albans*, written by Dame Juliana Berners about 1479.

Hedded lyke a snake
Nekt lyke a drake
Bakt lyke a beame
Syded lyke a breeme

Footed lyke a catte
Tayld lyke a ratte.

It is interesting to compare this version with Wynkyn de Worde's copy dated 1496. (*See* ORIGIN OF THE GREYHOUND.)

Periodicals: *The Greyhound Magazine* (published monthly) gives full coverage of the coursing, racing and show events.

The Greyhound Owner (published weekly) gives coverage of coursing and racing events.

Dog World and *Our Dogs* (both issued weekly) give coverage of all dogs in the show world – including the greyhound.

All these periodicals can be obtained from newsagents, but they may have to be ordered.

Placenta or Afterbirth: This is attached to the umbilical cord, through which nourishment and oxygen passes from the dam's blood to the foetus whilst it is growing in the womb. Each puppy is enclosed in a transparent envelope, from which the mother bites it free as it is born. At the same time, she bites free the umbilical cord from the placenta, thus cutting off the supply of oxygen from her body to the puppy's. She then licks the puppy, hard, all over not only to clean it but to start the puppy's lungs working so that they may take over. The placenta is expelled from the dam's body after each puppy is born.

Together with the envelopes, the dam eats the placenta; it is pure protein which nature first provided so that, in her wild state, it would sustain her and she would not have to hunt for food in the first stages of suckling puppies. This protein also acts as a strong laxative both for mother and puppies, and aids her milk supply.

Photo-finish, A Guide to: (Article by G. Peter T. Shotton, Racing Manager, Brighton & Hove Stadium, Sussex, which originally appeared in the *Brighton & Hove Stadium News*).

To understand how the photo-finish works, it is necessary to dismiss all preconceived ideas based on the principles of still cameras or cine-cameras. The photo-finish camera works in an entirely different way. It does *not* take a series of still pictures; it only takes one picture, but it takes this picture over a period of time.

The camera is mounted directly in line with the winning line and at right angles to the line of the course. Its position when it is installed is carefully surveyed to ensure this.

The ancillary equipment connected with the camera consists mainly of: (a) the spinner, (b) the timing equipment, and (c) the extra lighting. We will deal with these later.

The camera lens is masked by a slot. Through this slot the camera can see only the winning line – nothing else to left or right, just the winning line. When the camera is started, the film is moved horizontally across behind the slot in the lens at a speed which is proportionate to that at which an average greyhound crosses the winning line. Thus the moving film records, when nothing is on the winning line, a continuous picture of the winning line but, since the winning line is stationary and the film is moving, the winning line appears as a continuous blurred area all over the film.

When anything crosses the winning line it is recorded on the film; if it crosses from left to right at approximately the speed of an average greyhound it will be recorded clearly on the film, its speed being proportionate to that at which the film is moving. If one greyhound crosses the line, he is filmed not instantaneously, but in the time it takes for him to cross the line from head to tail. Each part of the greyhound is filmed as it crosses the winning line. Thus, if a greyhound puts one of his feet down on the winning line, this will appear blurred on the film since this foot will be practically stationary for an instant. If a greyhound is starting his stride as his front legs cross the winning line, the film may record him with an unnatural action. This is because his back legs will have moved by the time they are filmed from the position they were in when his front legs were filmed.

Thus, the photo-finish camera may give a distorted picture of a greyhound's action. What the job is intended to do is to decide which greyhound of two or more reaches the winning line first, and this job it does to perfection. Whatever anyone may tell you, whatever your previous ideas . . . the photo-finish camera *cannot* give the wrong result. If two greyhounds approach the winning line and their noses touch it together, their noses will be filmed at the same instant and will appear vertically in line on the film – a dead-heat. If one greyhound's nose touches the line before the others, the film will have moved between recording the winner's nose and the second's and the gap between the two vertically on the film will infallibly show this.

One thing that causes many headaches to people trying to understand this principle, and to those trying to explain it, is the vertical line that appears on the photo-finish print. This is *not* the winning line on the track recorded on to the film by the camera; it does not appear on the negative of the film at all. It is put there during the printing of the film, set at right angles to the direction in which the film was moving, to make it easier to distinguish which greyhound's nose was filmed first. This is done by a piece of wire set in the enlarger at right angles to the direction in which the film can be fed through the enlarger.

When making prints from the negative, the operator feeds the negative into the enlarger until the leading greyhound's nose is against the piece of wire; he then prints from the negative, and the piece of wire puts the vertical line on the print. The negative can only be fed into the enlarger at exact right angles to the wire; thus the nearer to the wire any greyhound's nose is, the earlier that greyhound's nose was filmed, and the earlier he crossed the winning line.

Once the whole principle is grasped it becomes clear that the camera cannot lie. It also disposes of the other arguments about the photo. One hoary old one is always cropping up. This is the idea that the camera takes the whole picture as the winner touches the line, and it is often said that the second greyhound on the film might have been passed by one of his rivals by the time the line was reached. This becomes ridiculous when one understands that each greyhound is filmed as he crosses the winning line and not before.

The 'spinner' we referred to is a disc rotating at the far end of the winning line from the camera. It revolves at the same speed as the average greyhound passes the line, and carries the name of the stadium, the date, and the race number, around the perimeter of the disc. As each figure or letter revolves past the winning line it is recorded by the camera, with the result that across the top of the negative, and of prints made from it, the name of the stadium, date and race number appear in a repeated strip; this gives an infallible identity to every negative and print.

The bank of lighting over the winning line is switched on at the same time as the camera and 'spinner', and provides the extra illumination necessary, ordinary track lighting being normally insufficient for the camera to record clearly.

The photo-timing is operated by a switch built into the starting traps. This starts a watch inside the camera; this watch is in the form of revolving drums of numerals and the camera records the drums on the bottom of the film at every one hundredth of a second. Thus the time recorded vertically below the winner was the time recorded at the same instant as the winner crossed the winning line, and so on with the remainder of the field.

We hope that this potted guide will serve its purpose, and clear up the many misunderstandings and misconceptions about the photo-finish which many people have.

Points of the Greyhound: The earliest type of greyhound seems to have

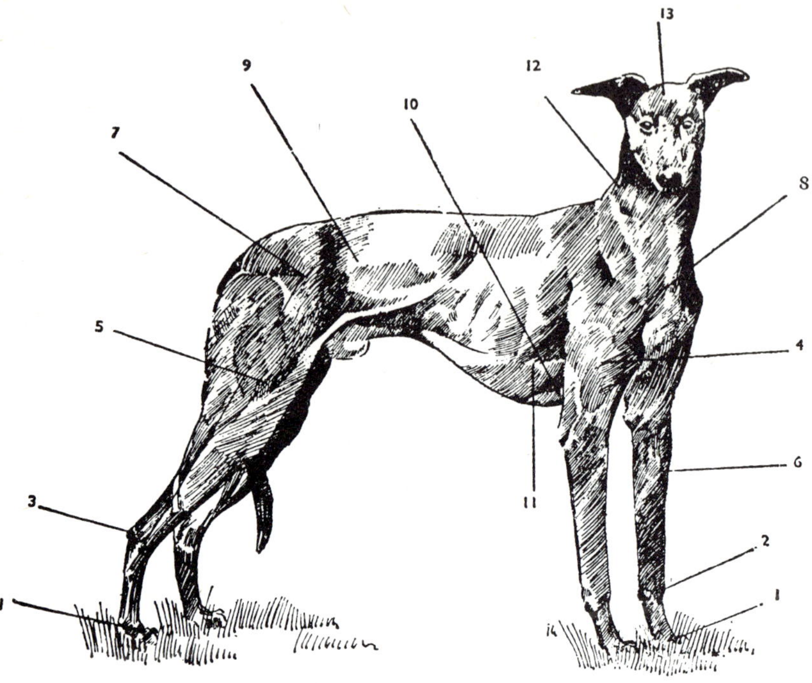

Fig. 8. Points of the greyhound

1. Standing on good feet
2. Wrists close to feet
3. Hocks well down
4. Bone strong and well-formed
5. Thighs well-muscled to give the necessary driving power
6. Forelegs straight, flat on the inside; muscular on the outside
7. Average length from hip to hock
8. Shoulders well-placed
9. Loins strong
10. Brisket deep and roomy
11. Well-set ribs with plenty of heart room
12. Neck like a drake; graceful in its symmetry
13. Head like a snake; long and tapering with a flat skull

been rough-coated. Even in the first pedigrees, early in the nineteenth century, greyhounds were sometimes registered as smooth-coated, and sometimes as rough-coated.

In the fifteenth century Dame Juliana Berners, the prioress of the Nunnery at Sopwell, and apparently a keen follower of the chase, is said to have written a book about the dogs of her time called the *Book of St Albans*. Her apt description of the greyhound, which has been passed down through the years might have been written only yesterday (apart from the spelling!). This description is also quoted in Wynkyn de Worde's *Treatise* (1496). (*See* ORIGIN OF THE GREYHOUND and PERFECT GREYHOUND.)

Today's typical greyhound has a flattened skull, fairly prominent eyes and a long muzzle showing plenty of strength. The ears should fall gracefully to the cheek, and never be pricked. It is true that, since racing came into being, there have been some very good 'trackers' with pricked ears, but this does denote a lack of quality in breeding and is something which would not be tolerated in the show greyhound.

The neck should be long and muscular, symmetrical and firm. It should be of sufficient length, and merge into sloping shoulders which give enough freedom to allow the dog to stoop to its quarry in his stride. The chest should be deep, and the under-part of the brisket fairly broad across. The formation of the sides (or chest) should afford plenty of heart and lung-room, with ribs well separated and more convex towards the quarters. Strong hind-quarters are essential in propelling a greyhound forward and these should give the impression of great power. The back should be arched, powerful and supple. 'Feet of a cat' gives the perfect idea of what the feet of a greyhound should be like; bones stout and strong, the claws thick and sturdy, and on perfect feet these seldom require cutting and are quite short. Since racing became popular, there have been many winning dogs with splayed feet, especially among the hurdlers, but this still doesn't alter the fact that there are still more injuries to badly formed feet than to those described. The 'tail of a rat' refers to the length of tail, sparsity of hair, and its whip-like quality.

Quite a few people have refused to buy a greyhound with a coarse tail, stating that the quality of a greyhound shows in its tail. The late Sqdrn Ldr G. R. Mack, MBE was always delving into the lore of the greyhound. He was one who would always first look at a greyhound's tail, saying, 'If it's coarse there's bound to be something wrong somewhere!'

Poisons and their Treatment: In all cases, very prompt action is required and you may save your dog's life by quickly getting him to disgorge what he has swallowed. These days, there may be better antidotes than washing soda, but they are not always to hand and, even if they are, can be disastrous if improperly administered; so a piece of washing soda (about the size of the top of one's finger) pushed down the dog's throat will be an effective emetic.

If poison is a liquid, the symptoms would show in a very short time – stiff limbs, difficulty in walking, spasms, etc., but something given in meat might take a few hours before the symptoms appear. Call your vet at once.

Poisons:

ARSENIC: Widely used in tonics – especially as a cure for persistent skin-trouble. A dog, because it has so much hair on its body, can safely take seven times as much arsenic as a human being but, if arsenic is given wrongfully or the tonic is carried on for too long a period, the animal can then suffer from poisoning.

Symptoms: The dog loses appetite and condition and, in chronic cases, becomes very weak and emaciated, and will vomit a frothy mucous as well as food.

Treatment: An immediate emetic is essential. Easiest to hand may be salt and water but, less distressing to the dog, is a piece of soda (twice the size of a hazel-nut for a fully grown greyhound) placed on the back of the tongue and gently pushed down with the fingers. This will cause the dog to vomit quickly. A laxative, such as Epsom Salts, should be given. Stimulants, such as brandy, may be necessary but as the dog improves milk, thickened with arrowroot, barley or rice may be given.

Arsenic should never be given as a tonic – *or in any form* – if the dog has any dressing on his skin which contains sulphur as combined arsenic and sulphur is a deadly poison to the dog. (*See* POISONS AND THEIR TREATMENT.)

LEAD (CARBONATE OF): Dogs have been poisoned by white lead but not often fatally unless swallowing pieces of the substance. For a long time, most paint contained white lead and a dog biting or chewing paint-work could easily have a serious case of lead-poisoning. Many old houses and buildings had water piped through lead pipes, which also could cause poisoning.

As lead is not a permissible agent in paint nowadays and lead pipes are not installed to convey water, the risk of lead-poisoning is slight. If lead water-pipes are known to be in use the taps should always be turned full on to run off any water which may have been standing in the pipes.

Symptoms: Vomiting, colic, pain (which is sometimes acute) and at first diarrhoea, which may be followed by constipation. Bad thirst, and sometimes paralysis of the hind legs and convulsions.

Treatment: Give an emetic at once to encourage sickness and a dose of Epsom Salts to stimulate the action of the bowels. Give plenty of fresh milk to drink – to which may be added the white of an egg.

Brand's Essence may be given frequently in small doses.

ZINC (OXIDE OF): Zinc in the form of lotion, powder or ointment is a good remedy for many forms of non-contagious skin trouble; but like most things applied to a dog's skin he likes to remove it as quickly as possible with his tongue. A small quantity may do no harm, but when the lotion or ointment is applied over a large area – and the dog licks a large quantity – serious disturbances of the system may follow. As a rule, acute cases are less fatal than the chronic ones such as in long-standing cases of skin-trouble when the zinc has been used daily for some time, and the dog has been consistently licking this. First effects of zinc poisoning would be the dog vomiting after food.

Symptoms: Great thirst and loss of condition and the dog refusing food altogether as sickness increases and becomes frequent. The dog is cold and dejected, and diarrhoea often occurs which adds to the weakness of the dog.

Treatment: Give a purge of Epsom Salts. Home-made beef tea in jelly form, or Brand's Essence, should be frequently given in small quantities or scraped raw meat – if the patient will take this.

Pores: Unlike the human being a dog has no open pores in his skin and perspires through the pads of his feet and the tongue.

Potatoes: After an illness, or when a dog is ready to resume training after a rest, a meal of mashed potato is very beneficial. It cleanses the stomach by removing any mucous or catarrh.

Prefix: (*see* AFFIX).

Pregnancy: (*see* FEEDING, NURSING and WHELPING).

Preparation for Racing: After a period resting from racing – whether the dog is above or below weight and he is likely to be above – he should be vomited, unless you are quite certain he has done this by eating grass. First thing in the morning, when the stomach is empty, give a small crustless slice of bread, and a minute or two afterwards slip a piece of common washing soda (*not* caustic) about twice the size of a hazel-nut down his throat and, within a minute or two, he will vomit, getting rid of any excess bile. The next morning, again on an empty stomach, give a large teaspoonful of Epsom Salts dissolved in warm water with a teaspoonful of honey to disguise the taste. About two hours later give a small meal of brown bread soaked in lots of warm broth which will cause the physic to act. If there is any sign of worms in the motion then the dog must be treated to destroy these (*see* WORMING).

Some years ago, a very successful greyhound trainer gave the author the recipe of a tonic, which he always used when preparing a greyhound for racing, after resting. First, worm the dog. Then, obtain from your chemist or druggist a bottle containing in *equal parts*: caster oil, Syrup of Buckthorn and Syrup of Rhubarb. First thing in the morning – after worming and on an empty stomach – give one tablespoonful of the mixture and reduce the dose to one dessertspoonful for the following six mornings. Syrup of Rhubarb is a wonderful tonic: we eat what grows on top of the ground from the rhubarb plant, but the real goodness is in the root.

The dog which is under-weight should be given a proportion of bread and meat which will increase his weight – more bread than meat. The dog which is over-weight should be given the same amount of food, but an increase of meat and less bread. Eggs, milk and meat build without fattening so, when the bread is decreased, the body will draw on the dog's own fat, to supply the nourishment needed. Thus neither the muscles, nor the digestion, become upset. When he has reached his correct weight, the proportions of meat and bread can be put back to the amounts necessary to keep the dog fit.

His increased walking and exercise will also begin to build his muscles. Work is a natural way of reducing fat and reaching a fitness peak, but a dog which has been inactive for any length of time must be put to work gradually – a fast or long gallop could ruin an unprepared dog. Road walking is the best exercise to start off with – five miles on the lead. On returning, the dog's feet should be washed in warm water to which a mild disinfectant or Condy's Fluid has been added and the feet and toes examined for soreness. If mud works under the quicks of the toes, a little vaseline (the yellow – not the bleached) should be applied and this will bring the mud away. When toes, or quicks, are very sore the best thing to use is the gentian violet spray, containing chloromycetin, which must be obtained from your vet, as it is on prescription. Be careful when using the spray, as dogs don't like the swish it makes and are inclined to gallop off if possible. The following day the dog should be allowed some free exercise on grass or turf, and also some walking on the lead.

As areas become more and more built-up, there may not be the necessary land for galloping, but there are plenty of parks around and it is always possible to find one where a dog may be galloped – if you get up early enough. When the dog returns, after his feet have been attended to, he should be massaged with hands and gloves, from his neck to his hind-quarters (*see* GROOMING).

The dog now needs strong short gallops, as well as road walking. The best way to gallop is for two to go with the dog – one to release him on a grassy slope (preferably uphill) and the other to go to the top of this and call the dog who should stretch right out. The dog should now be getting fit.

A greyhound's training exercise varies so much these days. Some trainers let them take all their runs on the track. Some walk the dogs for miles and others hardly at all. The best training must be that which gives the dog full exercise, but which gives a change from running round the track so that he does not become stale.

Prostrate Gland, Enlargement of: An operation for the enlarged prostrate gland in the older dog is not satisfactory, but sometimes castrating a dog suffering from this disease has a good effect. In this instance, of course, he cannot then be used for breeding purposes.

Proven Sire: When a dog, at stud, has his first litter registered.

Pulse: A dog's pulse varies in the number of beats per minute, according to his size. The number of beats is less in a big dog than in a small one. A St Bernard's pulse beats about seventy times per minute and a toy terrier about one hundred times per minute. A dog's pulse (unlike that of a human being) is intermittent in its beat.

In some cases of heart disease – or in pneumonia when the heart is affected – the pulse is very slow indeed. A big dog's may go down to fifty and a small dog's to seventy. A very slow pulse is more serious than a fast one. The pulse is always quicker in both young dogs and old dogs, than it is in those in the prime of life. The best place for taking a dog's pulse or heart beats is at the femoral artery, just where it crosses the inside of the thigh-bone.

Puppies: (*see* AGE FOR RACING, WEANING, WHELPING, WORMING).

Quarantine Regulations of Great Britain: The regulations prohibit the landing of any dog imported into this country from abroad (except from Northern Ireland, Eire, the Channel Islands or the Isle of Man) unless such landing has been authorized by a licence issued by the Ministry of Agriculture and Fisheries. Every such licence requires the detention and isolation of the dog for a period of six calendar months after the date of landing, upon premises previously approved by the Ministry for the purpose. The same requirements apply to a dog proposed to be landed from a vessel which has been in port outside Great Britain, Ireland, the Channel Islands and the Isle of Man (although it may not have been landed at such port) and also apply to a dog which has, at any time before or after arrival at a port in Great Britain, been in contact with any imported canine or feline animal. In no circumstances will the period of quarantine be reduced or the dog allowed to be detained and isolated in any manner other than that prescribed under the Order.

Any premises in Great Britain may be approved as a place of detention for an imported dog, provided they are in the occupation, or in the sole charge of a Veterinary Surgeon, and that they are considered by the Ministry suitable for the purpose of quarantine of particular dogs having regard to their breed and size. Before applying for the approval of any premises, an applicant should ascertain that the Veterinary Surgeon concerned is willing to receive the animal and to detain and isolate it in accordance with the requirements of the Ministry.

If you desire to obtain a licence authorizing the landing of a dog in Great Britain, application should be made on a form obtained from the Ministry of Agriculture and Fisheries, Animal Health Division, London. This form should be completed as far as possible but the application need not be delayed even if you cannot give the date and port of landing. The conditions printed at the foot of the application should be carefully studied before it is completed. One of the items to go on the form will be the name and address of the carrying agent selected to take charge of the dog immediately it is landed and convey it to the approved quarantine kennels. The carrying agent has to accept full responsibility for the movement of the dog direct from the port of landing to the kennels and may not give the dog to its owners.

If at any time during the prescribed period of quarantine you wish to transfer the dog from the premises in which it is being detained to other approved premises, or to a vessel for exportation, you should notify the Department of the Ministry of Agriculture and Fisheries of your wishes, giving as much notice as possible for the proposed transfer. A licence from the Ministry is necessary before such movements may take place, and all are required to be carried out by approved carrying agents.

The owner or importer of the dog at the time of importation must provide the Veterinary Surgeon in charge of the quarantine premises at which the dog is to be detained with a permanent address at which communications will at all times reach the owner or importer.

Rabies: Also known as hydrophobia, for the infected animal or person has a morbid dread of water. There is no cure for this disease and, once it is established, the dog should be destroyed at once.

The period of incubation is from two weeks to six months – but the average time is three weeks. Rabies can only be conveyed by inoculation – usually by the bite of an infected animal. The organism which causes the disease is present in the saliva, the urine and the tissues of the central nervous system of the affected animal.

The symptoms are those of most illnesses: loss of appetite and a rise of 2 or 3 degrees in the temperature. The dog may lick himself constantly where he was bitten. His disposition alters completely; a cheerful friendly dog will suddenly become morose and sullen and will, without provocation, attack both small and large dogs, and people too if they get in the way of the dog. The dog's voice alters, becoming half bark and half howl. Although he refuses food, he will bite through doors, carpets, kennels and almost any foreign object he sees. As the disease advances he becomes weak in the back legs, is eventually quite paralysed and, if not put out of his misery, usually dies within four or five days. Seven days is about the longest he can live.

Quarantine laws seem irksome and quite unnecessary to so many people – for who hears of a rabid dog? I heard of a man in India who had 'adopted' a little mongrel dog and both were inseparable, but the dog was rabid and bit his owner. Both died.

Racing, Origin of Greyhound: The first mechanical hare was tried out at the Welsh Harp, Hendon, near London in 1876 – but greyhound racing really first came into being when it was introduced in California. Greyhound racing did not make much headway in Great Britain until the Greyhound Racing Association opened their first track at Belle Vue, Manchester, in 1926. About a year later the White City Stadium in London, also a GRA racecourse, and the home of the Greyhound Derby, was opened. The opening of the impressive Wembley Stadium track (where the St Leger and the Trafalgar Cup are run) soon followed. In May 1928 came Wimbledon Stadium, the home of 'The Laurels' and The Christmas Vase, not forgetting the talent-finder of the young, the Wimbledon Produce Stakes, and the Puppy Derby and the Puppy Oaks. From then on greyhound racing flourished.

All tracks in England were closed at the outbreak of World War II, but soon opened up again with racing which, owing to black-out restrictions was held in the afternoons. The most profitable years must have been just after that war, when tracks seemed to be frequently filled to capacity. Today, tracks have to compete against a great many other sports, as well as television and off-course betting. Many stadiums have been sold for building development – for land which cost only a few hundred pounds is now worth many thousands. In or near London we have seen the closure of Charlton, Dagenham, New Cross, Park Royal, Stamford Bridge, Wandsworth, and West Ham stadiums. The provinces have the same story to tell. At the tracks still operating, vast improvements have been made and prize money greatly increased. It seems a far cry from the days when top dogs appeared in open races, running for a first prize of £10 – and £10 to the Red Cross!

Refrigeration: A refrigerator is necessary if large quantities of meat and other foods are to be kept fresh. If you live in the country, this can easily be run from a Calor gas cylinder. Food or drink should not be given to dogs direct from the refrigerator – but first left at room temperature for a time before feeding.

Registration: In America, show greyhounds need only to be registered with the American Kennel Club. Racing greyhounds are registered with the National Coursing Club. In England, show greyhounds must be registered with the Kennel Club, London. Coursing greyhounds are registered with the National Coursing Club, London – as are brood bitches, stud dogs and litters.

Any greyhound wishing to race under National Greyhound Racing Club rules has first to have been registered with the National Coursing Club. The rules state:

'Applications to register a litter of puppies must be received within six months of whelping and shall show the date of whelping and the name of the sire and dam. Applications must be accompanied by a certificate of mating signed by the owner of the sire and a statement showing the colour, sex, and number of puppies, which shall be verified by a certificate of a veterinary surgeon who has inspected the litter. The fee shall be £4 if the application is received within two months of the date of whelping; otherwise the fee shall be £10. No litter may be registered unless both sire and dam are properly registered, and the sire registered as a stud dog for the period during which mating took place. Any necessary corrections as to colour shall be made within six months of the date of whelping without fee, or after that time upon the payment of £1 for each dog, at the discretion of the Keeper of the Stud Book, who may ask for evidence in support of the application. In the absence of satisfactory support in writing the matter shall be dealt with by the Standing Committee. (*See* WHELPING.)

'No litter shall be registered if the application is received more than six months from the date of whelping, unless special permission shall be given by the Standing Committee. Every sire must be registered as such annually at a fee of £10, such registration expiring on 30 June in each year.

'Applications to register the name of a dog must include the month and year of whelping, name of the owner, colour (including detailed markings required on the forms authorized by the Keeper of the Stud Book), sex, and the names of the sire and the dam respectively. The name of the dog will not be registered unless the litter of which it was one has been registered. The consent of the Standing Committee shall be required to any application to name a dog made more than two years after whelping. The fees payable on the first naming of a dog shall be:

(a) £3 for each application received not later than fourteen months from the date of whelping.

(b) £5 for any application received thereafter – but within two years of whelping.

(c) £12 for any application received thereafter.

It is possible to transfer a greyhound from one owner to another so long as the National Coursing Club Re-Registration and Transfer Form is completed. Every change of ownership must be registered within twenty-eight days (for a fee of £4). After twenty-eight days, the fee increases to £6. If the name of the greyhound is also to be changed, an additional fee of £10 is due.

'The transfer form must be filled in and signed by present owner and new owner and the colour diagrams must be filled in on the back of the form.

'Any dog registered in the Irish Stud Book may be registered in the Stud Book for the purpose of registering a litter at the fee of £1, otherwise the fee shall be £1.50 up to the age of one year at the time of the application to register, or for any dog over one year of age the fee shall be £3 if bred in Great Britain, or £5 if bred in Ireland. Each application to register such a dog shall be accompanied by an Irish Coursing Club Identity Card (in cases where one has been issued) and an Irish Stud Book Certificate in the applicant's name.

'Any dog registered in any Stud Book (except the Irish Greyhound Stud Book) maintained by or under the authority of a recognized authority, may upon proof of such registration being furnished, be registered in the Stud Book at a fee of £5.

'Registration shall not be deemed to have taken place until the appropriate certificate has been issued by the Keeper of the Stud Book.

'Names of Dogs. No numerals will be allowed except to avoid duplication of a name already registered in the Irish Stud Book, this to apply only to

THE NATIONAL COURSING CLUB

82 BOROUGH HIGH STREET, LONDON, SE1 1LL

PARTICULARS REQUIRED FOR NAMING GREYHOUNDS IN THE GREYHOUND STUD BOOK

2

REGISTRATION FEES

For greyhounds registered by fourteen months of age	£1.50	each
For greyhounds registered thereafter up to two years of age	£3.00	each
Greyhounds over two years old can only be named by special permission of Standing Committee	£10.00	each
For registering Partnerships (in addition to naming fee)	£1.00	each partner

REGULATIONS

Registration must not be delayed until greyhounds are required to run.

Certificates cannot be sent per return post, AND WILL NOT BE MADE OUT UNTIL FULL FEES ARE PAID.

The insertion of the initials N.S. after an unregistered owner's name does not make his entry valid.

Rule 5 (II) The registration of dogs shall be made not later than the 31st May for inclusion in the next published edition of the Stud Book.

T. H. BALL, *Keeper of the Stud Book*

ALL CHEQUES TO BE MADE PAYABLE TO THE NATIONAL COURSING CLUB

Name of Greyhound	*Colour*	*Sex*	*Sire*	*Dam*	*Month and Year when Pupped*

As no numerals are allowed please give, in space below, several alternative names in case the first choice should have been taken.

Rule 42 Jurisdiction of National Coursing Club

Every person who is or was the owner or part owner of a dog registered under Rule 5 or who is or was licensed under Rule 44 and every person entering or running a dog or having the care, training, maintenance or superintendence of any dog or taking any part in any Coursing Meeting under the Bye-Laws and Code of Rules or making any application for registration to the Keeper of the Stud Book under this Code of Rules shall be deemed to have read the Bye-Laws and Code of Rules and to submit himself to the same respectively and to the jurisdiction of the Club and to consent to the publication to the Jockey Club, National Greyhound Racing Club, the Press and otherwise of any matter or decision under the Bye-Laws and Code of Rules.

I hereby authorise the above Greyhound bred by me to be named as the property of :-

(State Mr/Mrs/Miss) ....

Breeders Signature ....

Address ....

IMPORTANT *This form must bear the ACTUAL signatures of Owners and Breeders or their Authorised Agents. If this form is signed by an Agent, the written consent of the Owner or Breeder for such person to sign on his behalf must be lodged with the Keeper of the Greyhound Stud Book.*

Attention is drawn to the fact that the diagrams on reverse side MUST be completed in detail, and Certificate signed.

I declare that I have read the Bye-Laws and Code of Rules of the National Coursing Club and submit myself thereto and to the jurisdiction of the National Coursing Club and consent to the publication to the Jockey Club, the National Greyhound Racing Club, the Press and otherwise of any matter or decision under such rules.

PLEASE *Owner or Owners will SIGN here* .... *(State Mr, Mrs or Miss)*

WRITE *Full Address* ....

PLAINLY *Date* ....

COLOURS TO BE ABBREVIATED AS FOLLOWS :- Black-Bk / Blue-Be / Brindled-Bd / Fawn-F / Red-R / Ticked-T / White-W or any combination of these that may be necessary, the predominating colour being placed first.

Fig. 9 Registration form from the National Coursing Club

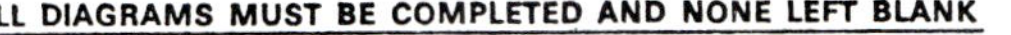

ALL DIAGRAMS MUST BE COMPLETED AND NONE LEFT BLANK

All special markings, scars, etc., must be entered in full detail on the above diagrams.

The Owner is responsible for notifying any changes or additions after Registration.

Colour of Eyes.................................

TOES

Mark colour of each toe, showing all white or light **by outline**

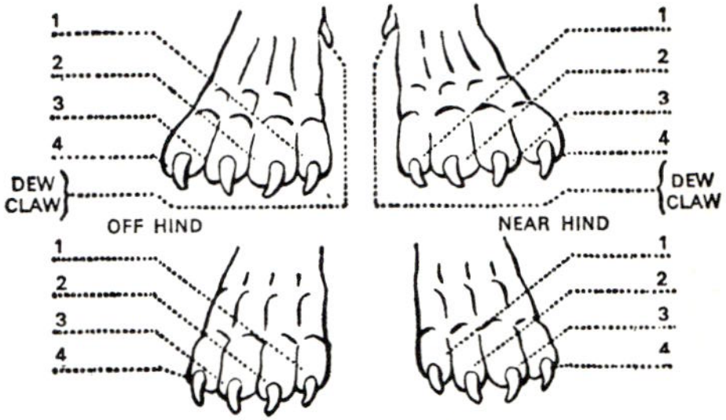

TOE-NAILS

Please mark Colour of toenails

D—**Dark**

M—**Medium**

L—**Light**

OFF FORE	NEAR FORE
1 in......out......	1 in......out......
2 in......out......	2 in......out......
3 in......out......	3 in......out......
4 in......out......	4 in......out......
5 in......out......	5 in......out......

OFF HIND	NEAR HIND
1 in......out......	1 in......out......
2 in......out......	2 in......out......
3 in......out......	3 in......out......
4 in......out......	4 in......out......

N.B.—Toe Nails are numbered as for Toes. IN is taken from *inside*, and OUT from *outside*, of Centre Toes.

I hereby certify that the particulars given on this form are correct

Owner signs here...

Date.................................

The actual signature of the Owner, or his Authorised Agent as notified to the Keeper of the Stud book, is required.

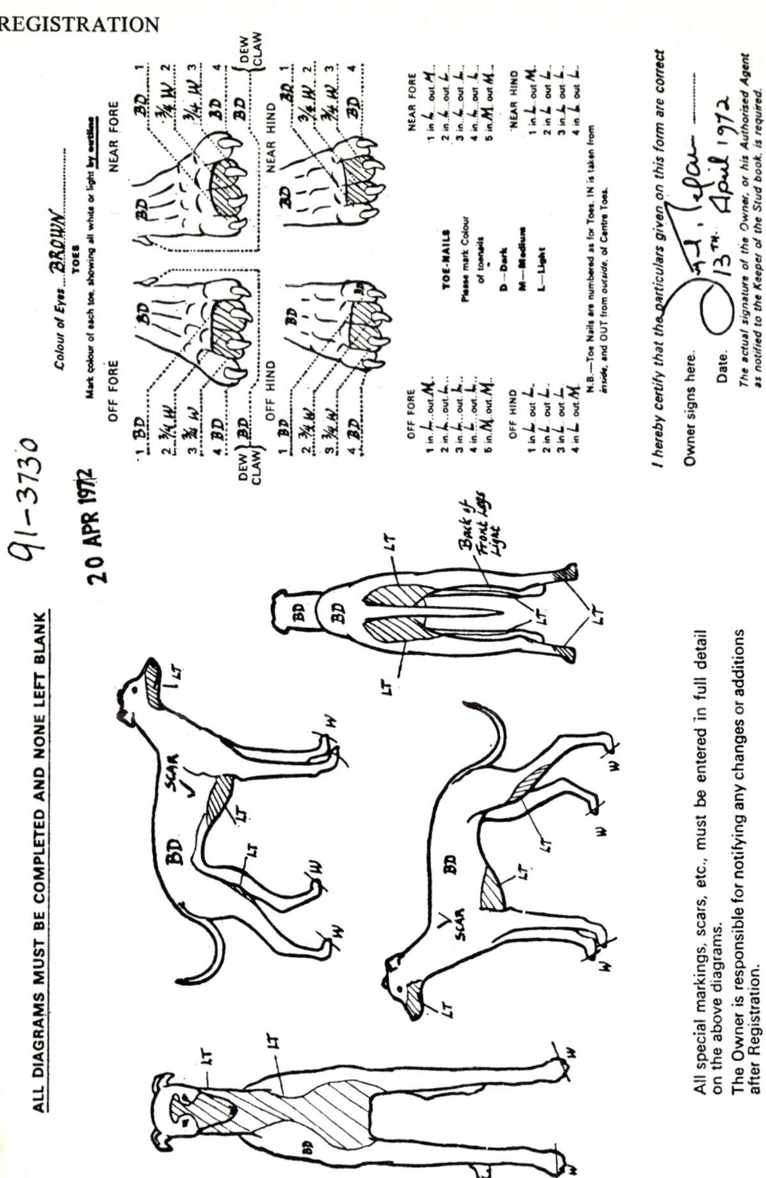
ALL DIAGRAMS MUST BE COMPLETED AND NONE LEFT BLANK

91-3730

20 APR 1972

Colour of Eyes ... BROWN

TOES

Mark colour of each toe, showing all white or light by outline

OFF FORE: 1 BD; 2 ¾ W; 3 ¾ W; 4 BD; DEW CLAW BD

NEAR FORE: 1 BD; 2 ¾ W; 3 ¾ W; 4 BD; DEW CLAW BD

OFF HIND: 1 BD; 2 ¾ W; 3 ¾ W; 4 BD

NEAR HIND: 1 BD; 2 ¾ W; 3 ¾ W; 4 BD

OFF FORE
1 in L out M
2 in L out L
3 in L out L
4 in L out L
5 in M out M

OFF HIND
1 in L out L
2 in L out L
3 in L out L
4 in L out M

TOE-NAILS
Please mark Colour of toenails
D—Dark
M—Medium
L—Light

NEAR FORE
1 in L out M
2 in L out L
3 in L out L
4 in L out L
5 in M out M

NEAR HIND
1 in L out M
2 in L out L
3 in L out L
4 in L out L

N.B.—Toe Nails are numbered as for Toes. IN is taken from *inside*, and OUT from *outside*, of Centre Toes.

I hereby certify that the particulars given on this form are correct

Owner signs here.

Date. 13th April 1972

The actual signature of the Owner, or his Authorised Agent as notified to the Keeper of the Stud book, is required.

All special markings, scars, etc., must be entered in full detail on the above diagrams.

The Owner is responsible for notifying any changes or additions after Registration.

Fig. 10 The above form filled in with colour particulars

dogs registered from the Irish Stud Book into the Greyhound Stud Book.

'A name once used will not again be available until ten years have elapsed from the date of registration of that name. The Keeper of the Stud Book shall have a discretion to refuse names held by former Waterloo Cup winners or other celebrated dogs.'

For registration of a racing greyhound with the National Greyhound Racing Club Ltd, London, the form has to be signed by a racing manager. All markings, colour, characteristics, etc., of the dog, required on the form, will usually be done willingly by an official of the stadium where the dog is to have its trials. These particulars and markings are then checked against those already given for registration at the National Coursing Club. Not more than sixteen letters may be used in the Greyhound's racing name, including spaces if of more than one word.

Retired Greyhound Trust, The NGRC: Formed to find homes for unwanted greyhounds retired from racing, sometimes through injury or other reasons, one of which is when a dog's racing days are over. The racing life of a greyhound is usually over when the dog still has many years to give as an affectionate companion; and an injury which may make him unfit for racing may make no difference to his life as 'one of the family'.

Money to help this scheme comes from many sources – including prize money from races arranged at various stadiums and sponsored races. The people who give their love, time and care to settle these dogs in happy homes ensure the scheme's success.

Rickets: A disease characterized by deformities of the bones and malnutrition. Sometimes it occurs through hereditary weakness but, commonly, through unhygienic surroundings and lack of freedom, fresh air and sunlight. Improper feeding, poor digestive powers, impoverished dam's milk and absence of the vitamins necessary for healthy bone formation are other causes. Treatment (preventative) should begin with the dam before the puppies are born. (*See* BROOD BITCH, FEEDING.)

Rugs: (*see* COATS).

Sapling, The: A greyhound at twelve months of age becomes a sapling and at thirteen months should be ready to have a hand-slipped trial. There is no doubt that the percentage of greyhounds lost to English racing today is far greater than that of twenty-five to thirty years ago. At that time, a puppy would be put in a trap (often home-made) on his home ground, for just two or three times, and allowed to run out to a rabbit skin either with meat in or as something to shake to his heart's content. Then he could go to any NGRC track to finish his schooling under the exact conditions of racing. A short handslip, then a longer handslip, and after a short solo run from the traps, he could go in with another dog, preferably with one that would lead for some way, and fade, so that the puppy could go by if he wished. This would be followed by a trial with an older dog who would not be too fast, but very keen for the 'dummy'.

Unfortunately, in England, these days are no more as far as the greyhound is concerned, for the tracks do not offer the same facilities to the young puppy at the most important time of his career. There are many good schooling tracks now, and they do a good job – especially for the puppy 'born to chase' – but some of the 'in-between' puppies need to be taught right from the first without variations.

A fifteen-month-old greyhound is called a young puppy. As regards racing he is young but in other ways he can be very wise, and has reached the age when he is aware of his likes and dislikes. Fully schooled on a private track, even with a noisy hare, he then has to learn all over again. Most of the NGRC tracks have extremely good facilities for their patrons, including built-in stands, restaurants, etc., which make a running hare present a completely different sound to the dog because of the various echoes. The traps, being electrically controlled and 'enclosed' by the surrounding buildings, have a loud buzzing noise to the acute hearing of the dog and, finally, he sees what appears to be a blazing light to run into at the photo-finish. It isn't surprising that some of them don't run as well as they do at home. If the young dog could be allowed to sample these obstacles from the very first, he wouldn't know there was anything different.

Apparently, a few years ago, there were too many greyhounds chasing too few races in Ireland, but the puppies were still all allowed to go to the racing tracks for schooling. Also in Ireland, as in Australia, they race under the open kennel system, so that puppies aged fourteen months do not have to be uprooted and taken from familiar to strange surroundings. They may go to much better surroundings and care, but to them 'home' is the place where they have always lived.

There are tracks in England – licensed by local councils but not racing under NGRC rules – where the dogs are taken to the tracks by their owners, raced and then taken home again. Many of these people would like to race under NGRC rules but just do not wish to part with their dogs.

Sawdust: Unless it is pine sawdust, it should not be used on floors where greyhounds are kennelled. It can cause sore feet and pads, and their feet are important.

Scottish Derby, The: Sponsored by Harp Lager, this race was run at Shawfield Stadium, Glasgow. The August 1980 final, with a first prize of £3,000, was won by Decoy Sovereign (F dog April 1978). Sire: Westmead County; Dam: Ka Boom. Distance of race: 500 metres. Time of race: 30.68 secs. Trained by: Joe Cobbold, Private.

Second was Coolarota (Bd dog Jan. 1978). Sire: Scarteen Dan; Dam: Flaxie. Third was Jon Barrie (Bk dog Jan 1977). Sire: Cashing; Dam: Famous Heart.

Seeding of Wide Runners in Open Races: In graded races, the seeding of wide runners has gone on for some time. These are placed in the outside traps to alleviate some of the trouble which may be caused by a wide runner coming from an inside trap. This is understandable as, before a dog is graded at a track for racing, he is given at least three trials with other dogs. The racing manager and those responsible for grading the runners, therefore, know the running style of the dogs before they are placed in the graded races.

Under NGRC ruling wide runners are also seeded in open races. For some time these runners were equally spread out in the heats, semi-finals, etc., of the major open races such as the English Derby, run at White City, London. As this system was found to especially favour wide runners the rule has recently been amended. It is now possible for up to six wide runners to be drawn together in these events, in the same way that it has always been possible for six 'railers' to be drawn together.

Sheath: If the skin and hair covering does not allow the penis to easily retract into the sheath after mating, this can be put right by a small surgical operation. In this case, consult your vet. (*See* COPULATION.)

Show Greyhound, The: The greyhound has been a native of Cornwall since ancient times. An old charter, under which certain lands are held in the Duchy of Cornwall, directs that a brace of greyhounds be delivered to the Duke of Cornwall as part of the terms of tenure. To this day the custom is carried out, but the greyhounds are always returned at the end of the ceremony.

Cornwall then – as now – was not a county as suitable for coursing as those in other parts of the country and has never been registered under the rules of coursing of England's National Coursing Club. Squadron Leader G. R. Mack, MBE, said that the earliest greyhounds in Cornwall were smaller than those in any other part of the British Isles. He stated as a fact that their present-day elegance could be attributed to a vicar of St Columb Minor, near Newquay in Cornwall who, in later years, owned a kennel of beautiful Scotch deerhounds. Apparently Cornishmen, who have always loved a lurcher as well as a greyhound, lost no opportunity in taking their greyhound bitches to St Columb Minor, to combine their blood with these handsome and graceful deerhounds. This may be the origin of today's show greyhounds.

The Cornish tradition is still upheld by such dogs as Mr Ralph Parsons' Ch. Rosyer-Poner (Best of Breed at Cruft's in 1971), and his young bitch Rafsyans-Plane – Cornish for Complete Rapture – (Best of Breed at Cruft's in 1972), both from his famous kennels at Wadebridge in Cornwall.

Mrs Judy de Casembroot, now of Somerset, is the breeder of the famous 'Treetops' greyhounds. 'Treetops' is a name known in all parts of the world. Many thousands of people who have never owned a greyhound will remember Ch. Treetops Golden Falcon as the winner of the supreme award of the show world – Best in Show, All Breeds, at Cruft's in 1956. He was only the second greyhound ever to take this coveted award; the other being Ch. Southball Moonstone of Haleyon, in 1934. Ch. Treetops Golden Falcon was a son of the wonder dog Ch. Treetops Hawk – the sire of thirty champions. The terrific impact of this sire in the greyhound show world is in evidence in many pedigrees, and in many countries, and will still be passed on through the years by his progeny. Through his descendants 'Hawk' has largely contributed to the present-day high grade of American show greyhounds.

Another beautiful specimen of a famous show greyhound is that of Ch. Boveway Yealver Theseus ('Boy' for short). He seems to depict every kind and beautiful characteristic of the greyhound, and came from the 'Ballymoy' kennels, at Bridge in Kent.

It is impossible to mention in this book all the achievements of greyhounds in the show world. They fully deserve the love and affection given to them by so many of their owners, who always seem to find a nook for them in retirement (which is where some owners in the racing world fall short).

Mrs Wilton-Clark, of Farley Hill in Berkshire, is known far and wide for her famous 'Shalfleet' greyhounds. Her beautiful brindled greyhound bitch Ch. Shalfleet Starlight was a prolific winner in Britain and, after emigrating to America, became Ch. Shalfleet Starlight of Foxden – a champion in both England and America. Two other Shalfleets have left England to become Champions in America – Ch. Shalfleet Spanish

Moon and Ch. Shalfleet Summer Magic, whilst the Shalfleets still in England continue to win.

The present-day show-bred greyhound is in most cases heavier than the champions of a few years ago, although according to the standard set down, the ideal height for dogs is 28 to 30 inches, and 27 to 28 inches for bitches. The weight, in some cases, is as heavy as 85 to 100 lb for dogs and 65 to 80 lb for bitches, and so much of the fine elegance of the famous greyhounds of a few years back seems to be disappearing.

Dame Juliana Berners, Prioress of the Nunnery of Sopwell, is accredited with a work in 1479 where she described the perfect greyhound (*see* SHAPE OF THE GREYHOUND). This has been passed down through the ages and, nearly five hundred years later, seems as applicable as it ever did. Harding Cox gave many interesting facts on what he considered the points to be taken into account when judging greyhounds, and these seem to be the same today, according to the leading authorities.

The head should be long and tapering, the skull slightly domed but flat where joining the neck. Ears small and well set. Eyes of moderate size – clear and intelligent. Muzzle long and strong, with pointed nose. Jaws level and muscular. Neck long and drake-like in formation, and graceful in its symmetry. Chest, though fairly flat, should be deep and roomy to allow scope for any extra strain born by heart and lungs. Shoulders long and well laid back to work smoothly on the flat surface of the ribs. Ribs well separated and more convex towards the quarters. Back arched, powerful and supple. Quarters should give the impression of great power. Strong hind-quarters are essential in propelling a greyhound forward. Thighs and gaskins should be well muscled. Stifle long, and well bent. Hocks well let down, and separated from leg bones. Forelegs should be straight, muscular on the outside but flat on the inside, with the bone carried well down. Pasterns long, but strong and springy. Perfect feet are cat-like, with well-knuckled strong toes. Tail is long and thin, sparse of hair, and tapering like that of a rat. Coat fine and close. All colours are permitted, including broken colours.

Unlike some of the other breeds, greyhound show entries have never been on a large scale although, at the present time, the entries have been much better and gradually more people are bringing greyhounds into the show ring. This is a good, healthy sign and augurs well for the breed. At the present time a few racing greyhounds are being quite successful on the show bench and some fine-looking dogs and bitches are competing in good company and winning.

The prize money does not encourage many racing owners to enter the show ranks, especially as the cost of food, travelling, etc., has soared so high.

Mr H. E. Gocher's famous dog Endless Gossip must have been one of the most versatile. A son of two English Derby winners (sire: Priceless Border; Dam: Narrogar Ann), he too won the English Derby in 1952, but then went one better by also winning the Welsh Derby. He won twenty-seven races, which included the Wimbledon Laurels, and then went on to run with great distinction in the coursing field. He ran brilliantly in the Waterloo Cup and, had he not been so hard-run in the fourth round, must have added this coveted trophy to his large collection. He then went to Cruft's, and was expertly handled in the ring by Mrs Idella Smith (an authority on greyhounds and whippets) and, although it was the first time he had entered the ranks of the show ring, he was good enough to have two nice wins to his credit – amongst all the show-bred greyhounds. Throughout his career he was in the care of the late Leslie Reynolds, trainer at Wembley Stadium. Endless Gossip was then sold to America, where he was successful at stud.

Mrs E. Richardson has kennels at 'Picket Twenty', Andover, Hampshire, and her greyhounds are noted for wins in the racing, coursing and show worlds. Miss Jane Lane, of Dorking, Surrey, also owns winners of races and show awards. They are also exceptionally clever – they know the shortest way home and the cosiest place to snooze when they decide their working days should be over! The greyhound bred for show purposes would not be improved by the extensive galloping and exercise so essential to its counterpart, the racing greyhound.

Walking will be more the main part of the show greyhound's training and exercise. Before the days of racing, it was quite usual for whelps at a very early age to be put 'out to walks'. In Cornwall, a butcher, a farmer, or a cottager, would take one or more greyhounds and train them and everyone, including the dog, was well fed – and the country lends itself especially well to the required development of the show dog. Short 'rabbity runs' were more the usual practice since, in Cornwall, there isn't the large and flatter type of terrain necessary for hare coursing. Many varied walks and exercise would be given to the greyhound. The proud Cornish 'walker' would take great care in moulding, feeding and caring for his charge; often standing the dog on a bench or table, putting one hand under his belly and gently raising his charge into a slight arch. Repeating this every day gradually trained the body of the pup into the necessary shape required in the show world – for the flatter back of the racing greyhound is not what is wanted on the show bench.

Although racing and coursing greyhounds, when puppies, are usually kept in a large paddock and can run in and out of a kennel night and day, the puppies bred for the show ring should be confined to their kennels for a period of rest at times.

The Greyhound Club is worth joining for information and interest regarding the show greyhound. Information can be obtained from the Club Secretary: Mrs D. Gilpin, 'Wenonah', 28 Old North Road, Longstow, Cambridgeshire.

Championship Shows which have classification for the breed are: Cruft's, Manchester, West of England Ladies' Kennel Society, Bath, Birmingham, Scottish Kennel Club Glasgow, Three Counties, Windsor, Paignton, Hound Association, Southern Counties, City of Birmingham and Ladies' Kennel Association.

Challenge Certificates are competed for at all shows, with the exception of Three Counties, Paignton and Southern Counties.

Show Greyhound in America: Many greyhounds have found their way from England to America – some of them via Cruft's – and this is evident from the pedigrees of a large number of American show greyhounds.

Bred and owned by Mrs Judy de Casembroot, of 'Treetops' fame, the English Ch. Treetops Hawk has shown in his progeny – including many champions in America and other countries – the great contribution he made to breeding. In the beautifully illustrated American periodical *The Gazehound*, Dagmar G. L. Kenis, of Los Angeles, California, wrote of Mrs de Casembroot, 'without whose greyhounds the breed would not be what it is today'.

Ch. Aroi Talk of the Blues, owned by Mr and Mrs N. J. Reese, was top dog in America's show world for 1979. This dog is now claimed to be the top winning greyhound of all time in the United States.

The top ten greyhounds in the American show world in 1979 were, in order of merit:

	owned by
Ch. Aroi Talk of the Blues	Mr & Mrs N. J. Reese
Ch. Rudels Rhapsody in Blue	S. Lackey & Dr E. S. Neustadt
Ch. Kingsmark Collage	W. Colby & J. Donaldson
Ch. Cyranos Ryal Brittania	D. Kelley
Ch. Huzzah Pursuit of Happiness	G. & J. Vaccaro & D. & S. Sprung
Ch. Ravendune Nickelodeon	C. P. & M. A. Maxwell.
Ch. Kingsmark Coffee Boston	B. S. Kendley & J. G. Donaldson

Ch. Huzzah Tiger Lily	P. Ide
Ch. Huzzah Lace Veil	B. Hickerson
Ch. Kingsmark Wish Upon a Star	J. G. Donaldson

Show greyhounds are registered with the American Kennel Club but racing greyhounds are registered with the National Coursing Club. (*See* REGISTERATION.)

Sire, Choice of: Of all characteristics for which a sire becomes your choice for your bitch, the chief of these should be speed. Puppies can be reared to attain staying-power but there must be speed as the foundation of their make-up – which it is hoped will be passed on to them.

Other characteristics are important and must be sought from the sire or dam, or from the combination of both. Courage is a necessity and basically means that a greyhound will pursue whatever his is chasing, as fast as he can and for as long as he can.

Jealousy is another essential quality for it means that the dog will run as fast and hard as he can, even though he may know he is only chasing a 'dummy' lure; for he intends to be first on the scene thus keeping any opponent from getting first 'look-in'. (*See* JEALOUSY.)

It is important that the qualities sought for your puppies must not only be obvious in the sire and dam themselves, but in their immediate relations. You may not find all necessary qualities in one of the parents and its family and this is where the knack in breeding comes in, by checking that any lacking quality may be counteracted by those qualities in the other parent and its family.

A poor litter costs as much, if not more, to rear than a good one, and breeding from nervous stock nearly always means it is the poor litter which will be your lot!

Greyhounds at stud are widely advertised in *The Greyhound Magazine, The Sporting Life* and *The Greyhound Owner,* etc., with their breeding and other information likely to be required, which owners or keepers will be glad to send.

A verse from Dryden – as quoted in *The Courser's Guide* (1896):

His age and courage weigh, nor those alone,
But note his father's virtues, and his own;
Observe, if he disdains to yield the prize,
Of loss impatient, proud of victories.

Skin Irritation: The dog may constantly bite, scratch or lick his skin, but often when examined there is nothing to be seen. It occurs mostly during hot weather and when the dog is shedding the old coat. For about a week give a daily dose of one level teaspoonful of Epsom Salts diluted in warm milk, to which has been added a teaspoonful of honey. Most dogs will lap this up. Bathe the dog in a tepid or warm solution of water to which one tablespoonful of Borax to each gallon of water has been added. On a warm day this is easily done in the garden by putting the solution into a bucket or bowl and then swabbing the dog all over – making sure that the liquid is squeezed out of the coat at the end.

Snake Bite: This hazard is only likely to concern dogs living in the country. The adder is the sole British poisonous snake. With a black and brown 'tweedy' skin pattern, he has a thick black V on his head. Like other snakes, he is deaf but picks up noises very quickly through vibration. He also has good eyesight. The adder is usually described as between 18 and 20 inches long. I once killed one which was over four feet long, but it was on ground which it loved – soft sandy soil, peaty woods, bracken and sunny paths, and acres of forestry with many a running stream to be found. For years the adders had lived there almost undisturbed. They are timid creatures, not vindictive, and will slink away whenever possible rather than attack. Greyhounds being as inquisitive as they are when anything moves do sometimes pay the penalty. Often, however, adders were found bitten up into small pieces and left as exhibits – so they didn't always win. The dogs are almost always bitten in the head or face.

As the venom produces a form of protein poisoning, protein should be cut out of the bitten dog's diet as far as possible; no meat should be given until the swelling has gone down.

First of all, give the dog a fairly large dose of Epsom Salts as this will help to clear the poison away. One level dessertspoonful of the salts should be dissolved in a little warm water and a greyhound will lap this up when a teaspoonful of honey has been stirred in. This dose should be repeated once more (after three days) and, each time, on an empty stomach. Feed the dog, on any cereal, such as semolina, rolled oats, groats or Benger's Food with milk added. Also suitable are rabbit, chicken or fish with brown bread or rusk soaked in the gravy – and bread and milk. However, as the patient won't feel he is suffering from anything – except food shortage – he will want plenty of this diet to sustain him. One thing to remember is that with an adder bite there will always be an abscess. It is usually easy to trace the source of the bite, where the swelling is worst, and hot fomentations should be applied two or three times a day. Take a flannel, or something woolly which will hold the heat, and wring it out in water as hot as your hands can bear. It is important to see that all the water is squeezed out, and then place the cloth on the swelling and hold there for a minute or two and repeat once or twice. Within a few days the abscess will burst. (*See* ABSCESS.)

Spaying: A bitch which has been spayed may race under NGRC rules – but it is not acceptable as an entry in any classic race, where dogs and bitches must be entire. Should you have a pet greyhound which may roam and come into contact with strays, the spaying of a bitch or the castration of a dog will make them incapable of breeding and prevent the unhappy problem of unwanted puppies. In either case consult your vet as it is important that the necessary operation be carried out by a qualified veterinary surgeon.

Splints, improvised: These may be of wood, cardboard or leather and are kept in position by bandaging. (*See* FRACTURES.)

Sponsorship of Greyhound Racing: During recent years, the welcome sponsoring of greyhound races has become rife: beneficial to the sponsor, in advertisement, and to the promoter, able to offer increased prize money to the competitors and top-class facilities to patrons.

1980 was the eighth year that Spillers had sponsored England's premier classic, the Greyhound Derby, where the final is run at London's White City stadium each year.

Amongst other things, Spillers is noted for the successful feeding of many thousands of English dogs. In this case, there may be an affinity between the sponsor and the sponsored.

Although on first sight of a greyhound most people think that it is likely to collapse through under-nourishment, they later accept – the greater the effort the larger the appetite, but still the graceful body. At the Derby presentation the winner, with his owners and handlers beside him, will usually show pleasure – for he senses that his human friends are pleased. But, if the £35,000 winner's cheque were presented directly to the dog, and he could speak, he would be most likely to say, 'I'd rather have a nice bowl of Winalot.'

Springbok Trophy: Run in February at one of London's GRA Stadiums. It is also known as the Daily Mirror Hurdles – for the race is sponsored by the *Daily Mirror*. An annual race for novice hurdlers, with a condition of entry that no competitor has won a race prior to 1 January.

The final of the 1980 Hurdles race (sponsored by William Hill) was run over the White City's 500 metres course.

Winner: Bobcol (Bk dog, Oct 1977). 2nd: Ballymena Moon; 3rd: Gilt Edge Flyer. Time of race 31.71 secs. Going: Heavy allowed 0.70 sec. Bobcol owned by Mr A. Felby. Trained by Miss N. McEllistrim. 1st – £1,000; 2nd – £350; 3rd – £200; other finalists – £70 each.

Standard for Greyhounds: By courtesy of the Kennel Club.

CHARACTERISTICS: The greyhound possesses remarkable stamina and endurance, its straight through, long reaching movement enables it to cover ground at speed.

GENERAL APPEARANCE: The general appearance of the typical greyhound is that of a strongly built, upstanding dog of generous proportions, muscular power and symmetrical formation, with a long head and neck, clean well-laid shoulders, deep chest, capacious body, arched loin, powerful quarters, sound legs and feet, and a suppleness of limb, which emphasize in a marked degree its distinctive type and quality.

Head and Skull: Long, moderate width, flat skull, slight stop. Jaws, powerful and well chiselled.

Eyes: Bright and intelligent, dark in colour.

Ears: Small, rose-shape, of fine texture.

Mouth: Teeth white and strong. The incisors of the upper jaw clipping those of the lower jaw.

Neck: Long and muscular, elegantly arched, well let into the shoulders.

Forequarters: Shoulders, oblique, well set back, muscular without being loaded, narrow and cleanly defined at the top. Forelegs, long and straight, bone of good substance and quality. Elbows, free and well set under the shoulders. Pasterns, moderate length, slightly sprung. Elbows, pasterns and toes should incline neither outwards nor inwards.

Body: Chest, deep and capacious, providing adequate heart room. Ribs, deep, well sprung, and carried well back. Flanks well cut up. Back, rather long, broad and square. Loin, powerful, slightly arched.

Hindquarters: Thighs and second thighs, wide and muscular, showing great propelling power. Stifles, well bent. Hocks, well let down, inclining neither outwards nor inwards. Body and hindquarters features should be of ample proportions and well coupled, enabling adequate ground to be covered when standing.

Feet: Moderate length, with compact well-knuckled toes, strong pads.

Tail: Long, set on rather low, strong at the root, tapering to the point, carried low, slightly curved.

Coat: Fine and close.

Colour: Black, white, red, blue, fawn, fallow, brindle, or any of the colours broken with white.

Height: Ideal Height for Dogs, 28-30 inches; for Bitches, 27-28 inches.

Note: Male animals should have two apparently normal testicles fully descended into the scrotum.

Stinging Nettles: The leaves of this plant, especially when young, are beneficial if made into soup and added to a dog's meal. I have known many greyhounds who pick and eat the leaves from this plant, from choice. Very rich in chlorophyl, the fresh leaves prevent dogs having a doggy smell. Blackberry leaves and grasses also serve the same purpose.

Stings: Bee or wasp stings cause redness and swelling of the part. The swelling will be much less serious if the sting is extracted. This can be seen easily at the seat of the swelling and can be extracted with a pair of tweezers. A sting on the tongue is the most serious.

Swab the swelling with diluted ammonia – which should be used sparingly – or with a solution of bicarbonate of soda and water; one tablespoonful to half a pint of water. If neither is available rub a piece of ordinary washing soda on the swelling.

'Stonehenge': This was the pseudonym of the author Dr J. H. Walsh. Editor of *The Field*, he was a prolific writer on the dog and was an authority on the greyhound. His first book, called *The Greyhound,* was published in 1853. This was described by the author as 'being a treatise on the art of Breeding, Rearing and Training greyhounds for public running: their diseases and treatment. Containing also, rules for the management of Coursing Meetings, and for the decision of Courses.'

'Stonehenge' was one of the original members of the National Coursing Club formed in 1857. From this date he was the editor of *The Coursing Calendar and Review* – soon only to be called *The Coursing Calendar.* This was originally published every four months, and there were many volumes before its termination in 1919 when 'Stonehenge' ceased to be editor. From this date the National Coursing Club issued its own *Coursing Calendar.*

'Stonehenge' was one of the original judges in the first officially recognized dog show, in 1859. In 1869 and 1875 two further books were written by him on the greyhound.

Stray Dogs: Where a dog has been taken to a police station, it should be claimed by the owner within seven days. If it is not claimed, the police may either sell the dog or have it destroyed.

Stud Card: When you have a dog at stud, it is usual to have an attractive card designed and printed which you can send to people who enquire about stud dogs. On one side of the card is given a resumé of the dog's racing or show career; his own breeding and any top dogs he has already sired. On the other side of the card you should display his name, colour, age, weight; the stud fee you expect and your name and address. It is a good idea to put the following line at the bottom: 'Return service only

GRAND RAIDER

GRAND RAIDER who had to retire from racing after only 16 race starts has started on a new career at Stud.

This brilliant son of the mighty Spotted Lightning will be well remembered in his short, but very impressive career.

He holds the 300 and 500yds records at Bathurst, won 4 races at Harold Park and was favorite for the Bi-Annual Classic in which he won his heat in 26.6. Between the heat and semi he broke down badly and was never to race again.

At Orange, he trialled 3/10 sec. better than the record which was held by the great Rocket Mac and he also equalled the Mudgee record in a trial.

GRAND RAIDER was surely going to be one of those freaks of Greyhound racing that we see burn up the tracks from time to time, but fate said no to this outstanding dog.

He comes from a litter that were 100% winners and three of his brothers, Free Quote, Silent Wish and Spotted Mate, all won races in the city.

GRAND RAIDER was bred by the Pringle family and they had so much faith in his father, Spotted Lightning, that they used him to produce the great Tara Flash and Arctic Light.

GRAND RAIDER'S mother, Estimate, was inbred to the great Top Linen, her mother Fine Finn is a sister to the mother of Best Sun.

There is no doubt in peoples minds who were close to this dog and knew his ability and fantastic temperament, that Grand Raider must produce top-class performers.

Fig. 11 Stud card

AT STUD **AT STUD**

GRAND RAIDER

Brindle Dog

January, 1967 **73 lb.**

STUD FEE $60 PLUS FREIGHT

Apply Lance Day, 17 Souter Street, Kogarah Bay, N.S.W., 2217

Phone: 54-2362

CONSIGN BITCHES TO KOGARAH STATION

RETURN SERVICE ONLY IF NOTIFIED THREE DAYS BEFORE WHELPING DATE if notified three days before whelping date.' Many breeders also show a photograph of the dog.

Stud Dog, Fee and Free Service: It is usual for the stud fee to be paid at the time of service. If the mating does not prove fruitful it is usual for the same bitch to be given a free service to the same dog. Although it isn't in the ordinary agreement regarding stud dogs, an owner will often let the bitch have a free service to another of his dogs or, alternatively, accept another bitch to the same stud dog.

The National Coursing Club certificates of registration of the whelps have, for some years now, been combined with the stud certificate by having this on the reverse side. No litter can be registered without this, and it has to be signed by the owner of the stud dog. This he may not be willing to do if the stud fee has not been paid.

Suppositories: Constipation, when wishing to avoid giving medicine by the mouth, may be relieved by passing a suppository made of glycerine and gelatine into the rectum. Failing a glycerine suppository, a piece of yellow soap cut in the shape of one, and well vaselined, serves the same purpose. Suppositories have the advantage over enemas in cases of paralysis, or severe illness, when a dog cannot stand whilst passing a motion. (*See* ENEMAS.)

Surfeit: (*see* ECZEMA).

Swallowing Foreign Objects: A greyhound has a big swallow and it is surprising what can pass down his throat and into his stomach. Unless the object is large and doing the dog obvious harm (when you must get in touch with your vet at once) it is best left alone. Feed him on stodgy food such as suet dumplings, rice pudding, bread, potatoes; this is to distend the bowels as much as possible, by causing large motions, and the foreign body will in all probability pass out safely. Do not give purgative medicines as they will cause contraction of the bowels and do harm. Treating a greyhound which had swallowed pieces of metal by chewing up a bowl, I found the best treatment was to give him a large suet dumpling (flavoured to his taste) every four hours. This follow-up system was more effective than one or two extra large meals. An X-ray showed that it had all passed out safely. Your vet will advise an X-ray.

Swimming: Most greyhounds love to go into water, and swimming is the finest exercise they can have since they exercise all the necessary muscles without strain.

Tail Bleeding: A tail which is bleeding at the tip is usually attributed to constant wagging and knocking the tip – but it is far more often a warning that skin trouble is on the way. It is a sign that skin trouble *will* come unless the matter is taken in hand. Although a dog has no open pores in his skin (as has the human being) there are certain conditions, such as over-heating of the body through wrong feeding (or an unbalanced diet resulting through the presence of worms) when serum will force through the skin. One of the most vulnerable places is the tip of the tail, where the skin is thin. Treating the dog internally is the quickest and safest way of dealing with this. The tail may be dipped once or twice a day in Proflavin emulsion (obtainable from chemist or druggist) or in a mild disinfectant well diluted with water. A light bandage may be put on this if necessary, but it is really better to leave it alone and not bandage.

Teeth: These are not visible when the puppy is born, although the milk teeth are already formed in the gums. The first of these usually show round about the twentieth day in a greyhound and, by the fifth or sixth week, he should have the complete set of twenty-two. The second and permanent set usually comprises forty-two in number. At about four months of age the puppy starts to lose his milk teeth, and the permanent ones start to appear. Bitch puppies often cut their teeth a little earlier than dogs, and winter puppies take slightly longer to cut their teeth, as they do to open their eyes.

Puppies, from the time they are weaned, should be given bones to gnaw. They must be large non-splintering (such as marrow bones) and it will often stop the puppies eating stones and other hard objects, which they seem convinced should be part of their diet (*see* BONES). Hard biscuits or dry rusk are good substitutes. These should keep the teeth in good condition and they may need no other attention.

If tartar appears on the teeth, as the dog gets older, this should be removed as it will damage the teeth and they may eventually become loose. A good teeth scaler can be bought but a small nail file, with pointed end, will do equally well. Be careful not to injure the gums; insert the point carefully under the edge of the gum where it meets the tooth and scrape gently down. Once free from tartar the teeth may be kept clean by a soft brush dipped, first, in warm water and then a little tooth powder, but *not* carbolic. Loose teeth should be removed and sometimes, in an old dog, it is necessary to remove all the teeth. The dogs seem to get on quite well without them and their gums, eventually, become quite hard. Teeth should be taken out by a veterinary surgeon, who will give the dog an anaesthetic so that he knows neither pain nor fear.

Temperature: The normal temperature of the dog is 101.5°F. To take the temperature, an ordinary blunt-edge thermometer should be used (as supplied by the chemist or druggist for human beings). For dogs, the end of the thermometer should be inserted into the anus and held there carefully for one minute. See that the mercury is completely covered.

Dogs' temperatures, taken before leaving their own kennels for the journey to the race track, would give a good indication of their well-being or otherwise.

Tendons: Injury is most likely to be found in racing greyhounds because of the strain on their legs when running at speed. This is most serious when tendons on the front feet, behind the wrist, are affected.

Symptoms: A degree of swelling will be seen in the tendon or tendons, the part will be painful when touched and the dog is likely to show lameness.

Treatment: Foment the swelling, with a pad of cotton wool by first wringing it out in hot water and placing on the leg for a few moments, and then doing the same with cold water. Repeat several times two or three times a day for two days. After this, put the dog's foot only in cold water; preferably by taking the dog to a stream where the water is very cold, or using a hosepipe on the foot. Failing this, put the foot in a bucket of water – the colder the better. Carry out this treatment until all swelling has disappeared. If one has access to a swimming pool – or the dog can go in the sea – there is no finer treatment for any lameness in the greyhound than swimming, for the dog receives exercise without any strain on the limbs. The dog should be kept to walks on the lead only but these may be increased as the lameness goes.

There is a surgical operation which can be carried out by a qualified veterinary surgeon when tendons are badly damaged, whereby an incision is made and the tendon allowed to be loose after being cut. Then the incision is sewn up and left to heal. This operation I saw carried out on three racing greyhounds but, although they returned to racing for a time, their speed was sadly diminished. It is only fair to say that the dogs would possibly never have been able to race again without this operation, but I would never have another done.

Toe, Bruised: This is best treated by keeping the dog on a lead for exercise and immersing the foot in very cold water or playing a hose on it, once or twice a day. Your vet may think it advisable to 'cut-back' the toe nail to relieve the pressure.

Toe, Dislocated: (*see* DISLOCATIONS).

Toe Nails: These should be kept short and trimmed with a reliable pair of nail clippers when necessary. Make sure that the claws are not cut back as far as the quicks as this would be painful to the dog and make him wary and difficult next time. Most toe nails show a definite line where the quick starts, but since this is not easily seen in the black toe nail, a little at a time should be taken off. One can then judge where the quick starts.

Track-Leg: A name applied to a form of lameness in greyhounds, due to the constant strain of turning at high speed on the sharp bends of the racing track. It would not apply to the greyhound used only for show purposes; and it is unusual in the coursing greyhound, because he twists and turns after the live quarry – unlike the track greyhound which always runs the same way round. Just before the last war – which prevented the experiment being thoroughly tested – the GRA was arranging to stage races on right-handed tracks, instead of always on the left-handed, as it was thought that this could counteract some of the lameness to which racing greyhounds are prone. Further, it was thought that a wide-runner on the left, would be a railer on the right.

Symptoms: A slight swelling appears just above the inside of the hock and, when pressure is applied, the dog flinches and may show lameness. In fact, it is only these symptoms, and the fact that the swelling is soft, that show it is track-leg; for many legs can show a slight enlargement here but this is simply due to the hazards of racing and the swelling is firm when touched and gives no trouble.

Treatment: Foment with alternate hot and cold water for the first two or three days and then with cold water. (*See* TENDONS.)

Tracks: (*see* RACING, ORIGINS OF).

Trafalgar Cup, 1979: The final of Wembley's blue riband of the puppy races was won by Trina's Girl. Whelped in October 1977. Sire: Myrtown; Dam: Trina Ceili. Over a distance of 490 metres the winner's time was 29.53 secs. The bitch is owned by Mr A. Hillman. The trainer was Mrs Wearing (Bletchley).

Trainer of the Year: Greyhound Racing's award for 1979 went to Geoff De Mulder, who won the same award in 1978. Among his many stars is Sarah's Bunny, winner of the 1979 Greyhound Derby. The presentation took place at the London Hilton, in April 1980, at a dinner and social evening organised by the breeders' and trainers' associations. The 1979 award winning Oscars were also presented to the owners of the winning dogs: Desert Pilot, Gay Flash, Kilmagourna Mist, Sarah's Bunny and Weston Star (*see* OSCARS, 1979).

Travel, by Air: There is a very prompt and efficient air service to and from England's Heathrow Airport and Ireland's Dublin Airport, which is extensively used by greyhound owners. Each greyhound travels in a separate crate, similar to a racing trap, and there are no quarantine laws between these two countries. Many greyhounds travel to other countries by air and, although in many cases the dogs do not have to go into quarantine on arrival, they must do so – for six months – if returning to England.

In Australia it is illegal for *any* dog to arrive by air. Dogs arriving by sea have to go into quarantine in Australia, but only for seven weeks, as the time spent on the voyage also counts.

Today, in modern aircraft, the atmospheric pressure in the cabins is kept the same as the atmospheric conditions at ground level.

Travel, by Rail: Greyhounds, other than puppies, have to be muzzled when sent on a train journey. The dog must also have a chain – not a leather lead – attached to the collar. If the weather is cold he needs a coat. The dog is then placed in the care of the guard of the train, and is put in the guard's van with his chain arttached to an iron ring. Greyhounds sent on a train journey are usually taken great care of by the guard. A small puppy may be sent in a crate and, again, will be looked after by the guard. Forms have to be filled in, and these are obtained from the parcels office of any station. Labels attached to the dog's collar, with address of his destination, should be securely tied.

Travel, Preparations for: Nausea and vomiting do affect some dogs when travelling by sea. Your vet will give you a sedative, or tranquillizer for a dog going on any journey, if necessary, but in my experience they travel much better without this. Having sent greyhounds to Australia and India by sea, to Ireland by air, and many on train journeys in Great Britain, including young puppies, without any form of tranquillizer, I found that they all reached their destinations safely and in good condition. In each case I was told that they arrived without any signs of fear or distress.

On several occasions I did, however, have dogs sent to me which arrived seeming abnormally docile and vague but, after some hours in their new surroundings they seemed to 'come to' and seemed very distressed and nervous. On making enquiries I found that, in each case, the dog had been given 'something to keep him quiet on the journey'. Unlike human beings, a dog cannot anticipate fear in any form of going on a journey. It is up to the one who sends the dog on his journey to see that he is put in the charge of a reliable person – for one is always handy. I have found that employees of air, rail and sea services are extremely kind to dogs which travel. A greyhound loves to be with people and usually quickly adapts himself to any circumstance when he meets them. Finally, no dog should be given a meal immediately before travelling.

Trespassing: The owner of a dog is not answerable in trespass for its unauthorized entry into another person's land, but a man is liable for trespass if he wilfully sends a dog on to another's land in pursuit of game, or if he allows a dog to roam at large knowing it to be addicted to destroying game. Where a tespassing dog causes damage by killing or injuring livestock, the keeper of the dog is liable for the damage caused. Furthermore, although to shoot or injure another man's dog is an actionable wrong, the owner of livestock, or a person acting on his behalf, may justifiably shoot a dog if: (1) the dog is worrying or is about to worry livestock and there are no other reasonable means of preventing or ending the worrying or (2) the dog has been worrying livestock, has not left the vicinity, is not under the control of any person, and there are no practicable means of ascertaining to whom it belongs.

Tumours: A local swelling in any part of the body, usually from a morbid growth. A tumour may be malignant or non-malignant but, in certain cases, the latter may become malignant. Malignant tumours are progressive; they spread their roots as they invade, destroy the tissues and break up healthy blood vessels. Operation in the early stages of the disease may be successful.

Non-malignant tumours, although they may grow very large, do not encroach upon surrounding tissues of the body and, in all stages of this tumour's growth, an operation for its removal is usually successful. (*See* CANCER and MAMMARY GLANDS.)

TV Trophy Race BBC, April 1980: The televised final of this race was run over 850 metres flat at Wembley Stadium. Tread Fast (F dog May 1977) was the winner in 53.20 secs. Sire: Glin Bridge; Dam: Edenvale Lady. Trainer: Sharp of Walthamstow Stadium. Prize money: £2,000.

Uterine Inertia: When labour pains do not fully increase to the required force for the birth of the puppies. Letting the bitch loose in the paddock surrounding the whelping shed may put this right, or a ride in a car or van on a bumpy road or uneven surface will usually induce the arrival of the puppies. If these measures are not successful, your vet should be called and he will give her an injection which should put matters right. Greyhound bitches rarely have a Caesarean operation as they do not have the birthing problems of the bitches of smaller breeds.

Vagina, Discharge from: Bitches sometimes suffer from a white discharge from the vagina before, but more often after, 'being on heat'. In the first case, just keep clean by occasionally sponging the external part with a weak solution of TCP and water. When it occurs after the 'heat' means must be taken to stop the discharge, as it can be very weakening. Take advice from your vet. Sometimes after whelping a litter, the bitch will continue to discharge a thick, dark-looking blood for weeks; this causes weakness and can upset the milk. If this continues for much longer than a week, consult your vet. Keep clean by wiping with clean cotton wool which has first been wrung out in warm water (which has already been boiled). Dry the part and, if sore, wipe it gently with a very small quantity of olive oil or vaseline. No strong smelling additive should be used since puppies find their mother by smell.

Vagina, Injuries to: Although a puppy may arrive naturally, injury sometimes occurs during the birth or the vagina can be injured by dragging apart the dog and bitch during mating when they are 'locked' together. This is quite unnecessary as they will separate themselves in due course. If any accident occurs during mating, such as falling, they can be separated if the dog's testicles are gently but firmly pressed. In an ordinary case of injury to the vagina, the passage should be washed out night and morning, using a syringe with a long nozzle and a warm solution of permanganate of potash or with a solution of boracic acid. In either solution, one grain should be used to an ounce of water. Injuries during whelping are more serious, as there is a danger of blood-poinsoning (when the bitch would show symptoms of a very high temperature, loss of appetite and vomiting). Your vet should be called.

Value Added Tax: Before any greyhound is imported into the United Kingdom, most likely from the Republic of Ireland, a special form declaring the value of the import has to be completed by the British importer. This valuation has to include all costs and charges incurred up to the time of reaching the port of entry into the United Kingdom.

Through negotiation by the National Greyhound Racing Club with Customs and Excise officials, agreement has been reached on the acceptable values for greyhounds other than those which already have a market value when VAT charges can be assessed accordingly.

For greyhounds reared in the Republic of Ireland for UK owners:

A puppy not over ten months old, £30 plus the cost of carriage and insurance to the UK.

A sapling not more than sixteen months old, which has not raced or had trials up to the time of being imported, £50 plus the cost of carriage and insurance to the UK.

These values are agreed – providing the dog has not been purchased immediately before importation, or that a price previously paid does not exceed the above values.

Forms are obtainable from: Collector's Office, Customs and Excise, from the main ports of entry into the UK; also from all NGRC race-courses and from Ireland's Bord nag Con, Shelbourne Park, Cork and Limerick.

Vermifuge Enema: To use after worming a dog and after the worm medicine has had effect and worked the bowels. Copious enemas of water (temperature 100° to 101°F) will help to ensure that any worms remaining in the lower bowel are brought away. To each pint of water, add one teaspoonful of common salt.

Veterinary Certificates: These are required by some countries, especially when a dog is exported to a country where livestock is extensively bred, as in Australia. (*See* QUARANTINE.)

As conditions covering the entry of a dog by another country vary from time to time, it is advisable to get an up-to-date form, with the latest information required, from the Ministry of Agriculture and Fisheries if you wish to export a dog.

Certificates are required for other reasons:

To be given to the racing manager of any track racing under NGRC rules when a trainer has to withdraw his greyhound from a race in which he was entered.

To be sent to the NGRC each month, by all trainers registered with the Club, to show the condition and well-being of greyhounds in their charge.

At the time of the registration of all litters of puppies (at eight weeks of age) verifying their age.

All dogs registered under Kennel Club rules must be examined by a veterinary surgeon before being granted admittance to a dog show.

There are many other reasons, such as when a greyhound is sold, or changes hands.

Veterinary Surgeons: A veterinary surgeon examines each greyhound due to race at a meeting at least one hour before racing starts when the dog is presented for kennelling. He will not pass any greyhound which may have been dressed with any substance which could be absorbed through the skin. Nor will he pass a greyhound which, in his opinion, is unfit to race.

All trainers, under NGRC rules, know a good vet, for he will have to visit their kennels at least once a month for the necessary report which has his signature before going to the NGRC.

Should you have only one dog, perhaps a pet, you should know the nearest reliable vet, for you never know how quickly you may need him or her.

Vitamins: These are found in food and it is better for the body to receive them through a balanced diet rather than over-dosing one vitamin by pills or injections, which can diminish or destroy the other vitamins in the body. Over-dosing of them all can cause vitamin poisoning.

The over-heating and cooking of foods does destroy more vitamins, so it is sometimes necessary to replace these. Bemax, given daily, is one of the best sources of vitamin B as it is easily sprinkled on food and the dogs like it. Another source is liquid Cytacon, obtainable from any good chemist or druggist. Vitamin C is present in citrus fruits. There are tablets obtainable which contain each, or all, of the vitamins. These are reliable but it is always better to give a course of, say, one month and then stop doing so for a time. If necessary another course can be given later.

As a guide, here is a list of vitamins and some of the foods in which they are present:

VITAMIN A: Promotes growth, tissue formation, and aids digestion. Natural sources of Vitamin A are milk, butter, cheese, cod liver and other fish oils, green vegetables, potatoes, carrots, spinach, eggs, green peas, beans and bananas.

VITAMIN B: All cooked foods are deficient in this vitamin – either partially or fully – according to the degree of heat and time of cooking to which the food is exposed. Deficiency in this vitamin impairs the appetite and digestion and results in both loss of weight and vigour. Its absence can cause paralysis of some muscles and can develop a tendency to diabetes and nervous disorders. General sources of vitamin B are cereals, peas, beans, raw fruit, buttermilk, cabbage, corn, spinach, honey and egg yolk.

VITAMIN C: Necessary to the well-being of skin and joints. Its absence brings about eczema, and an addition of sufficient quantities of vitamin C to the diet will cause the subsidence of this complaint. Sources of vitamin C are green foods, oranges, lemons, tomatoes, raw fruit, potatoes, milk, liver and raw cabbage.

VITAMIN D: Regulates mineral metabolism and controls calcium equilibrium. The chief source of this vitamin is sunlight, and growing animals should be given as much freedom as possible in the light and the sun. Deficiency in vitamin D causes muscular weakness, lack of resistance to infectious diseases, rickets, bone deformities and defective development of teeth.

VITAMIN E: Is necessary for reproduction in both sexes, and its deficiency causes sterility. It is the vitamin necessary to feed the other vitamins in the body. Main sources are wheat germ, milk, lettuce, watercress and fresh fruit.

VITAMIN G: For growth and development. Main sources are cereals, brains, yeast and eggs.

Vomiting: Sometimes a husky cough can be caused through excessive bile, since a dog cannot remove this by spitting or clearing his throat when it distresses him. Vomiting in the dog is a natural process and he will do this for himself whenever he can by eating certain grasses. The favourite sort is the very coarse grass which he will eat and later regurgitate; blackberry leaves and stinging nettles have the same effect. If he has no access to grass then there is a very simple and harmless way to help him. On an empty stomach, give him a slice of soft bread to eat, without crust. A minute or two after he has comfortably swallowed this, take a piece of common soda (not caustic) about twice the size of a hazel-nut and open his mouth, gently putting the soda on the back of his tongue and pushing down with the finger. Within a few minutes he will regurgitate bread and soda, thereby ridding himself of any excessive bile. If the vomiting was very necessary, what he returns will be of a dark brown to saffron colour, otherwise just yellow to white. In any case it will benefit him to have removed the bile.

Unless you know that a dog vomits himself with grasses, it is as well to do so with soda about every three months. It is surprising how often the 'grass-eaters' do this for themselves. Never artificially vomit a dog if he has swallowed anything sharp or bulky. (*See* SWALLOWING FOREIGN OBJECTS.)

Waterloo Cup: The blue riband of coursing was first run in 1840 at the famous Altcar coursing ground and from then on was a yearly event until 1974. 12 February 1974, was to have seen the start of the one hundred and thirty-fourth Waterloo Cup, at Altcar in the north of England, but owing to a water-logged course, mainly through an essential drainage scheme being incomplete, it had to be cancelled for the third time in the last seven years. After being cancelled in 1947 and 1963 the Cup was run, in both cases, in the autumn of those years.

Run at Altcar, the 1973 Cup was won by Modest Newdown, when he beat High Executioner in the final course. Modest Newdown is a son of the famous Newdown Heather, sire of so many winners in the racing and coursing fields, and his dam is Modest Millie.

The 1975 Waterloo Cup was won by Hardly Ever. In the final Course he beat Hollypark Magpie.

Hardly Ever (Rf dog June 1972): Sire: Cons Duke; Dam: Dendera Lena. Owned by Mrs Ellis of Cirencester. Trained by Charlie Howard.

The 1976 Cup was won by Mrs M. Ryan's Bd dog, Minnesota Miller (Sire: Bright Lad; Dam: Latesia). Henry Tudor ran up.

The 1977 Cup was won by Mrs M. Ryan's Bd dog Minnesota Yank (Sire: Bright Lad; Dam: Latesia). Cookie ran up.

Since 1977 the Waterloo Cup has not been run, but it is not to be phased out. The President's Cup meeting substituted in 1978 for 32 all aged. Won by Countess Fitzwilliam's Rf dog Milton Ruff (Sire: Linden Eland; Dam: Tendring Ita).

Waterloo Cup, America: 'The first American Waterloo Cup was started on 8 October 1895 with the meeting commencing on Tuesday and being concluded on the Friday. This was the tenth Annual Meeting of the American Coursing Club and, in addition to the Waterloo Cup, Purse and Plate being decided, an additional stake called the American Coursing Derby for sixteen puppies was added.' (From *The Courser's Guide* (1896).)

A course meeting of this size is no longer held in America.

Weaning: If possible, the milk given to puppies on leaving their dam, should be goat's milk. It is very nourishing and, as it is naturally homogenized, easily digested. It is very important in a greyhound's life that, when leaving his dam, the food given him as a replacement for her milk, should be easily assimilated. Upset digestion at this stage of his life can cause malnutrition (which also means lack of growth), rickets and skin trouble. Cow's milk is the next best thing to goat's, but should not be diluted, as bitch's milk is so much stronger in fats and casein than this (*see* MILK). From four to five weeks the puppies may have gruel made from Robinson's Groats, sweetened with a little honey or glucose, and a little scraped raw meat (starting with a teaspoonful each once a day). As the bitch will have to be taken away at intervals if the puppies are too boisterous, she should be left with them at night if possible, and allowed to feed them some time during the day.

As soon as the babies are old enough to waddle out of their kennel they should be allowed to do this; if the step from the kennel is too high a pile of straw should be put here so that they may scramble in and out as they wish. When her puppies first come out, the dam will run around the paddock letting them follow her, until she stops dead. She will do this, gradually increasing the distance she runs with them behind her. She knows what she is doing, and will stop when she thinks they have had enough. It is this which develops their lungs and chests and makes them stayers in later life.

At the sixth or seventh week the bitch may only be feeding them at night, although she may stand and let them have a little milk during the day. At this time she should be back to only two meals a day. After these meals she will want to go back to her puppies and should be allowed to do so. She will then vomit some of the food she has eaten (which will be partially digested) and the puppies will be ready to eat this. At seven weeks of age, it is wise to look into the worming of the puppies (*see* WORMING).

At seven weeks old the puppies should have four meals a day. Below is only a rough guide to these as the food the dam is giving them will have to be taken into account:

First meal between 6 and 7 am. Wholemeal or Hovis bread soaked in warm milk with a half-teaspoonful of Virol or honey allowed for each puppy. Or give the milk to drink and dry rusk to eat. Or gruel made from Robinson's Groats, Farex, porridge (this in colder weather) or semolina, and the Virol, honey or brown sugar added.

Second meal between 11 am and noon. Stale wholemeal bread soaked with gravy until moist, with scraped raw meat added. A little Bemax may be given with this.

Third meal between 4 and 5 pm. As the second meal, but with cooked meat from sheep's head, or fish, rabbit with milk.

Fourth meal between 9 and 10 pm. As the first meal – or baked custard slightly sweetened. Leave the puppies with pieces of dry rusk to chew. All soaked bread or rusk should be moist but not sloppy.

Puppies should always have access to water. At sixteen weeks the puppies should have three meals a day. Similar meals may be given but more meat allowed. Now raw scraped carrots may occasionally be given in the food, raw chopped cabbage stump sprinkled on the food; onions in the gravy and portions of garlic segments alternatively given raw. From six months of age *see* FEEDING.

Web, Split: This occurs quite frequently in racing or coursing greyhounds. Although the web (between the toes) may only have a slight split, it is very difficult to heal. Stitching is sometimes satisfactory but most veterinary surgeons eventually decide to cut the web right up to the farthest point. This does give extra play on the toes, which they would be better without, but there doesn't seem to be an alternative.

Weight, Racing: An NGRC rule demands that the racing weight of a greyhound must not vary more than 1 kilo either below or above his previous racing weight. When the weight variation exceeds this the greyhound is withdrawn from the race by the stewards at the meeting.

Weights and Measures: (Helpful in the use of medicine).

60 drops or minims	1 drachm
1 drachm	1 teaspoonful
2 teaspoonfuls	1 dessertspoonful
4 teaspoonfuls	1 tablespoonful
2 tablespoonfuls	1 ounce
8 drachms	1 ounce
8 teaspoonfuls	1 ounce
20 ounces	1 pint

Teaspoons vary in size; the correct one to use may be obtained from any chemist or druggist.

A 4-ounce bottle of liquid mixture contains 8 tablespoonfuls, 16 dessertspoonfuls or 32 teaspoonfuls.

Welfare of the Greyhound in Transit: People connected with establishments where racing greyhounds are housed are fully aware of the strict supervision necessary, twenty-four hours a day, to protect the dogs from outside interference.

A very vulnerable place is the van or vehicle used for transporting the dog to a race or trial. The van should always be thoroughly wiped out before putting the dog into it and, even then, he should be muzzled with a box-muzzle, unless he has a handler with him throughout the journey.

When the van is left in a stadium's car park, it should still be guarded, especially if the greyhound qualifies in a heat or semi-final of a race, and is returning for the final.

A drug concealed in a substance which the greyhound will eat can make sure that the dog's next race will be run entirely different from its known form. It isn't only a depressant drug that ensures a dog will lose his race; it can be something quite the reverse, which will energize and over-excite him but, in a day or two's time, resulting in lethargy.

Whelping, Preparation and Procedure: When the puppies are due to be born, some symptoms will be noticed, and the bitch may be disinclined to take her food. As a rule she starts to scratch and make her bed and, as the labour pains come, is restless and pants, often looking round and licking herself. The puppies are then likely to be born within an hour or so; a first litter sometimes takes longer than a later litter but, as already stated, parturition is easy in the greyhound and there are seldom whelping troubles. If, however, you are in any way worried, telephone your vet who will always give reassurance, but he would be the first to agree that bitches, when whelping, are best without strangers around unless it is really necessary. She will be pleased to see someone she is used to, especially if it is a first litter, and will appreciate a drink of warm milk, to which a little honey or glucose has been added, between the intervals of the puppies arriving.

When all the puppies have arrived, wipe her hindquarters clean with a flannel or sponge wrung out in warm water (do not use disinfectant) and dry with a soft towel. Bitches which have had their puppies easily do not require much food for the next twenty-four hours. The foetal envelope, in which each puppy arrives, is eaten by the mother, as is the afterbirth. An animal in its wild state receives enough nourishment from this to be able to stay with its litter for three days without food. As it is pure protein, it is essential that the mother is not given meat and other foods rich in protein too soon. For the first day after whelping, gruel made with milk and Benger's Food, Slippery Elm, Robinson's Groats or something similar may be given two or three times a day, and also milk to drink and water should always be available.

On the following day she may have gruel and also boiled fish, with the bones removed and mixed with cooked semolina or something similar, or mixed with uncooked Farex. A sweetened egg custard baked in the oven will also make a change. On the third day she may have cooked rabbit, some rusk crumbled with this and the gravy until it makes a moist, but not sloppy, meal. She now needs to go back on to meat, which may be built up to the quantity required. Raw meat is the greatest producer of milk and, cut small, easily digested by the bitch. She may also have the flesh and gravy from sheeps' heads mixed with rusk, to make a moist feed. The meat may sometimes be cooked to make a change.

Sometimes, after whelping, the bitch has diarrhoea, but as a rule it is not severe and should pass off in about twenty-four hours. If it goes on for longer, a dessertspoonful of castor oil should be given and, if necessary, her milk thickened with arrowroot. If she has a large litter, it will be better to give her food in three meals as she will need a continuous quantity of good noursihing food.

The greyhound is a wonderful mother, and is often reluctant to leave her litter, but she should be encouraged to go into her paddock and later, when she will leave them for a little longer, she should be taken for short walks. The greyhound dam, being rather thin-skinned, has quite a lot to put up with from the babies' claws and teeth. The little white hooks at the end of the claws should be cut off with scissors when they are ten days or a fortnight old. At three weeks of age the puppies may be introduced to a dish of warm milk sweetened with honey, or Nestlé's milk. Dip your fingers in this and they will suck them and then gently coax them to the milk. They all start off the same way – crawl in it, roll in it, and then all sit down and suck each other, until the mother returns to give them a bath. The health and well-being of young puppies can be seen, and felt. They visibly grow and should be firm and strong when picked up and, if the mother is caring for them and feeding them well, it is better not to introduce artificial feeding too soon. Their stomachs, at this age, are ready to digest what their mother gives them – strong nourishing milk which contains everything they need – provided she is well-fed and cared for.

As the puppies move about in the nest, it should be seen that the boards dividing the bench are high enough to prevent the puppies scrambling over to their mother, when she wishes to rest from them.

Before the puppies are six months old, they should be registered with the National Coursing Club. The fee for the registration of a litter is £2 providing the application is received within two months of whelping; thereafter the fee is £10. No litter is accepted for registration in the Stud Book after six months from the date of birth without special permission of the Standing Committee. (*See* REGISTRATION.)

Whelping Quarters: The paddock should be at least three-quarters of an acre large, fenced in by strong link wire. This should be six feet high bent inwards at the top. An ideal paddock slopes towards the south, with a hedge on the north side as a protection from winds.

The hut, far enough inside the paddock to allow puppies to run around it, should be about twelve feet by twelve feet, and six feet high, with the entrance on the east side which will give protection from gales. Inside the building, a partition should run from north to south for nine feet – this will leave a three-foot passageway to the screened off compartment. On the north side should be the bench, and windows of glass on the south side to give plenty of light. These windows should be made to open as the sun may be hot in summer and dogs need plenty of air, although never draughts.

A door is necessary whilst it is being used as a whelping shed, but later it may be taken away or put on a latch and always left open so that the puppies may run in and out as they wish. So built, winds will be prevented from blowing on the bench. The shed should be lined with wood to four feet up, and no cracks or crevices left anywhere for draughts to penetrate. The sloping wooden roof, and the outside of the shed, should be covered with roofing felt.

The bench should stretch across the whole width of the hut, nine feet, having allowed for the passageway. From back to front the bench should be about four feet deep – allowing plenty of room for a growing litter of puppies – and about six inches from the floor, but this space should be blocked in whilst the puppies are small enough to get underneath. A board along the front about eight inches high will keep any bedding in. The bench should be of wood, and the floor should be made of wood as well. Puppies, and young dogs, may have plenty of room on a bench, but that won't stop them from often piling on top of each other and sleeping on the floor. There is no doubt that just as lack of light is a great contributor to rickets, so is the use in kennels of corrugated iron and concrete, which causes rheumatism. The bench and floor in the kennel must be completely flush; no open or cracked grooves to get little toes and feet caught in.

This bench will be too large for whelping and tiny babies. The usual type of whelping box with open front flap may be put on the bench; but it is a better idea to divide the bench by putting a board down the centre, about nine inches high. The bitch will often like to lie away from her puppies on the other side of the bench after feeding them. It is important that a wooden rail, a few inches above the floor, be put around the whelping compartment of the bench. Should a puppy crawl behind its mother she will not crush it when she leans back as it will be pushed under the rail and so protected.

Good clean wheat straw was at one time used for the bedding but, today, is unobtainable (*see* BEDDING). In any case, whatever the bedding, the dam will scrape it all away and place her babies on the bare boards which are very warm, so she might just as well start off this way. It is easy to keep the bed clean and easy for her to clean up the evacuations of the whelps, which she will do for at least three weeks. Wood is warm and if the kennel is constructed as recommended, there should be no artificial heating unless the weather is very cold. The bitch runs a temperature when the puppies are born, and her body gives off a great deal of extra heat to keep the babies warm. Good nourishing food will do the rest. If a brood bitch leaves her litter looking poor and thin, then she has not been looked after properly. She should be well and have a 'good back'; and the only time she will look thin is just before the puppies are born. when her backbone will appear to stand up a little.

Wimbledon Classic, The Laurels: Winners since its inception (the distance being 500 yards):

Year	*Winner*	*Trainer*	*Track*	*Time (secs)*
1930	Kilbrean Boy	Orton	Wimbledon	29.20
1931	Future Cutlet	Probert	Wembley	28.52
1932	Beef Cutlet	Hegarty	Cardiff	28.47
1933	Wild Woolley	Campbell	Belle Vue	28.80
1934	Brilliant Bob	Orton	Wimbledon	28.46
1936	Top O'the Carlow Road	Orton	Wimbledon	28.39
1937	Ballyhennessy Sandhills	Orton	Wimbledon	28.25
1938	Ballyhennessy Sandhills	Orton	Wimbledon	28.50
1939	Musical Duke	Crowley	Park Royal	28.42
1940	April Burglar	Appleton	West Ham	28.56
1941-1944	Not run			
1945	Burhill Moon	Orton	Wimbledon	28.42
1946	Shannon Shore	Reynolds	Wembley	28.26
1947	Rimmels Black	Biss	Clapton	28.77
1948	Good Worker	Daley	Ramsgate	28.49
1949	Ballymac Ball	Martin	Wimbledon	28.61
1950	Ballymac Ball	Martin	Wimbledon	28.19
1951	Ballylanigan Tanist	Reynolds	Wembley	28.37
1952	Endless Gossip	Reynolds	Wembley	27.96
1953	Polonius	Reilly	Walthamstow	28.04
1954	Coolkill Chieftain	Harvey	Wembley	28.05
1955	Duet Leader	Reilly	Walthamstow	28.25
1956	Duet Leader	Reilly	Walthamstow	28.23
1957	Ford Spartan	Hannafin	Wimbledon	27.89
1958	Granthamian	Harvey	Wembley	28.57
1959	Mighty Hassan	Harvey	Wembley	28.01
1960	Dunstown Paddy	Reilly	Walthamstow	28.02
1961	Clonalvy Pride	Harvey	Wembley	27.66
1962	Tuturama	Sanderson	(Private)	27.83
1963	Dalcassion Son	Hiscock	Belle Vue	28.08
1964	Conna Count	Hannafin	Wimbledon	28.08
1965	Conna Count	McEvoy	Wimbledon	28.13

Year	*Winner*	*Trainer*	*Track*	*Time (secs)*
1966	Super Fame	Gleeson	Wimbledon	28.05
1967	Carry On Oregon	Orton	Wimbledon	27.89
1968	Ambiguous	McEvoy	Wimbledon	28.10
1969	Ardine Flame	Kinsley	Wembley	27.96
1970	Sole Aim	Geggus	Walthamstow	28.04
1971	Black Andrew	Singleton	White City	27.96
1972	Cricket Bunny	Booth	(Private)	28.11
1973	Black Banjo	O'Connor	Walthamstow	27.93
1974	Over Protected	Coleman	Wembley	28.00
1975	Pineapple Grand	Baldwin	Perry Barr	27.77
1976	Xmas Holiday	Rees	Wimbledon	27.66
1977	Greenfield Fox	Dickson	Slough	27.26
1978	Jet Control	Gaylor	Perry Barr	27.45

World Greyhound Racing Classic: Known as the 'Super Bowl' of Greyhound Racing – with prizes money of $125,000 – was run at America's Hollywood Greyhound Track. This multimillion stadium is deservedly described as the Palace of the Greyhound Racing Industry. The largest track in the world, it is exclusively used for greyhound racing.

The 1980 eight-dog final was run in March. The first prize of $33,000 went to Banker Hop, owned by Daryl Brumage and trained by Don Cuddy. Second was Kunta Troubles and third was Jimmy's Smile.

It is unfortunate that WGRF members, Australia, Ireland and the United Kingdom, find it impracticable to compete in the World Classic, due to the quarantine laws of these countries. A greyhound returning from America would have to spend six months in quarantine and would then need further time to reach peak fitness after the long rest.

Many owners of greyhound racers find it hard to understand why horses are allowed to travel freely, without quarantine restrictions, whilst the dog must be subject to them. The greyhound's racing life is very much shorter than that of the horse.

World Greyhound Racing Federation: The purpose of the WGRF is to act as the co-ordinating and discussion forum for the representatives of the controlling bodies of all countries where greyhound racing is promoted as a national sport. The Federation was first formed in 1971 and comprises representatives from the greyhound racing controlling bodies in countries where the sport is contested, i.e. Australia, Great Britain, Ireland, Mexico, Spain and the USA. The members of the WGRF are the controlling bodies of the above six countries which are as follows:

Australia – Greyhound Racing Control Board, New South Wales

Britain – National Greyhound Racing Club
Ireland – Bord Nag Con
Mexico – Comision Nacional De Carreras Y De Galgos
Spain – Federacion Espanola Galguera
USA – American Greyhound Track Operators Association.

The offices of the WGRF are at 139 SE 14th Lane, Miami, Florida 33131, USA.

Worming: If possible, the worming of puppies should be left until they are eight weeks old. After dosing, they then have the power to expel the dead worms more easily than very young puppies. Raw eggs included in the diet will keep the worms at bay, but sometimes puppies have to be wormed before they reach this age. Worms always seem to be present in new born puppies, despite the precautions taken with the dam before their birth. Your vet will supply you with the necessary worm medicine, and there are some very good remedies supplied by reliable chemists or druggists; but always read the instructions for administration carefully.

On the day before worming (unless you are given any other instructions) feed the puppies at their normal times by giving them sloppy meals of bread and gravy, biscuit and gravy, or boiled fish and gravy. Leave out the late night feed, and early the next morning give the medicine, as instructed. One hour after worming is completed, give each puppy half a teaspoonful of castor oil in a little warm milk or gravy. One hour later, give them a warm sloppy meal of bread and gravy. Then carry on feeding normally. The dosing may have to be repeated in ten days' time, if instructed to do so.

Young dogs never seem to be without worms for long, and they need dosing periodically as they tend to be listless when worms are present. Round worms are especially lowering as they multiply quickly and apart from those in the bowel, they find their way to the stomach and other parts of the body. As these parasites (whether round or tape worms) take the best of the nourishment from food eaten by the dog, the dog's diet soon becomes unbalanced. In all cases, staring coats and voracious appetites are sure indications that worms are present in the dog.

For getting rid of the tape worm in adult dogs (more often found in the adult than the young dog) there are many preparations on the market, which can be obtained from your druggist or chemist. Or, as with the puppies, a vet will give you the necessary dose – with instructions. Feeding, on the day before worming, will be the same as for the puppies, but a larger meal will be required. An hour after worming, the dose of castor oil should be one dessertspoonful. Most dogs will take this readily if given in a little warm milk.

The author has found that there are two things worms do not like to live with. One of these is garlic and the other orange juice. Dogs receiving these through their diet, will often expel worms without having to be dosed for this.

The garlic bulb is made up of segments, and a segment chopped and added to the dogs' food will keep worms away. Alternatively, some segments may be boiled in the dogs' cooked food. Most greyhounds will readily eat half an orange or take some orange juice on their food. Virol (obtainable from all chemists and druggists) is extremely good for both puppies and adult greyhounds, and can be given alternately with honey on the breakfast. One of the ingredients of Virol is orange juice.

Wrist: Damage here is likely to recur. It shows by the wrist swelling through strain or wrenching.

Treatment: (*see* TENDONS). No exercise other than walking until all inflammation has disappeared. Wrist trouble must be given a long time to recover before the dog is put back into training. Putting him to work too soon may then cause irreparable damage.

Zinc Poisoning: (*see* POISONS, ZINC).